THE MAN WITHOUT A MATE COOKBOOK

Reviewer Comments.....................

"...This cookbook enables anyone to prepare a delicious meal without having to think about it!"
Peter, 23, Premed Student

"...I am really impressed with the format. Organizing menus, with grocery lists and time schedules, is exactly what most cooks take a long time to figure out."
Joanne, 54, High School Home Economics Teacher

"...These recipes stuck to the basics, making cooking an easy form of entertainment for me and my lady guests. They were amazed I could cook and doubly amazed that it was good!"
Jim, 28, Employment Counselor for the Disabled

"...This unique cookbook brings easy success to every user, no matter how inexperienced. It demonstrates that cooking and entertaining build relationships."
Geri, 56, High School English Teacher

"...The menus are excellent! By following the shopping lists, you know what to pick up without taking much time. The recipes are very simple to follow and enable an amateur to have professional results."
Dave, 31, Corporate Benefits Consultant

"...This cookbook is the best thing for the single male cook since Dustin Hoffman (Kramer vs. Kramer) showed us how to make French toast! By following the step-by-step methods to simple, satisfying meals, you gain the added bonus of feeling good about yourself."
Judy, 46, Graphics Director

"...It's great! It's precise and easily understood. For a noncook like me, this is the ticket for an excellent home-cooked meal. I especially liked the shopping lists!"
Larry, 50, Farmer

"...This cookbook is unique! It's written in user-friendly language for the beginner, but offers menus that won't bore the advanced. The variety of menus will help one progress from being intimidated by the kitchen, to becoming a confident gourmet."
Christine, 23, Information Systems Specialist

"...I enjoyed it! The recipes are a pleasant adventure in cooking and provided some good-tasting meals."
John, 64, Retired Business Executive

"...It's not often you go through a cookbook and go, Ya! Ya! Ya!"
Pamela, 37, Office Business Manager

THE MAN WITHOUT A MATE COOKBOOK

The Successful Lifestyle Cookbook for the Unmarried Man

BY BOB LUNT

A Successful Life Alone Cookbook

GARBORG'S

P.O. Box 20132 / Bloomington, MN / 55420

THE MAN WITHOUT A MATE COOKBOOK

The Successful Lifestyle Cookbook for the Unmarried Man

BY BOB LUNT

Published By

Garborg's Heart 'n Home
P.O. Box 20132
Bloomington, MN 55420

Publisher's Cataloging-In-Publication Data
Lunt, Robert D.
The MAN WITHOUT A MATE Cookbook
1, Cookery. 2, Self-Help. 3, Autobiography.
TX714L91   641.0   91-66424
ISBN 0-9630296-3-0

Printed in the United States of America

The Man Without a Mate Cookbook

Contents

THE MAN WITHOUT A MATE COOKBOOK

CONTENTS, *continued*

Author's Acknowledgments

The idea for this cookbook originated several years ago. But other people and other things were always in the way of getting started. Yet, in spite of time and circumstances, the idea persisted. I began to realize that there was a "Divine Calling" on my life to write this book.

As I got started I was able to find the right people at just the right time. I virtually did not have to leave my zip code area to find who or what was needed to accomplish this work! Amazing! Amazing Grace!

I began by sharing my idea with Lois Kemp, Certified Home Economist, Byerly's, Inc., and asking her for technical assistance. She recommended Betsy Norum, CHE. Betsy, in turn, enlisted the aid of Joan Miller, CHE. I cannot thank them enough. Not only for their creativity and professionalism in preparing the menus and recipes contained in this cookbook, but for their moral support and encouragement.

Midway through the writing Betsy became very ill, so Joyce Gauck, CHE, joined us in editing the menus and recipes and assisted Joan in developing the index. Credit is also due Deidra Schipani, Regional and Seasonal Cuisine, for her assistance with many of the flavored-coffee suggestions.

Stacy Turos, Science Museum of Minnesota, saved the day (and me) with her word processing skills. David Farr, ImageSmythe, did the cover design, Vicki Schwartz created the illustrations and Jean McKenzie Johnson edited the personal text. Finally, I want to express my gratefulness to Nathan Unseth, a friend whom I called on frequently for reality checks and guidance as to what to do next. He quickly became my "Father Superior."

A special word of appreciation is due to a host of friends who provided an unending supply of encouragement and support. Clearly, no man stands alone. This production has become something of a community project; one that we have accomplished together, but for which I'm solely responsible.

To

My family, who have suffered through many meals that were not quite what they were intended to be.

From Burnt Offerings to Melted Hearts

I went from my mother, to my wife, to McDonald's. Then, as a consequence of a broken marriage and my teenage children making their home with me, I needed to cook. But I was not a cook, and cookbooks intimidated me more than the Scriptures.

I discovered that cookbooks were written by cooks, for cooks. They were technical publications that required professional training to read, let alone use. What did "cream" the sugar and shortening mean? And, what on earth was a jelly roll pan?

It wasn't long before my women friends (who I thought were cooks by nature) began to tire of my panic-stricken calls and questions, most of which they could not answer! I found cooking a frightening and frustrating experience. But the real frustration was trying to put together whole meals. What goes with what?

And, guess what? I also found that cookbooks were basically written around a particular food item (e.g., bread, mushrooms, etc.), or around a special cooking technique (e.g., wok cooking, microwave cooking, etc.), or contained a jillion gourmet recipes for everything under the sun. But no menus for whole meals.

I needed menus, shopping lists, and finally, recipes for weekend and holiday meals with my children, or for a dinner for two, or for meals when I was alone. In short, I needed a cookbook designed around my lifestyle, rather than around a special cooking technique or a particular food item. It needed to be simple, easy to read and understand with no technical jargon.

Hence, *THE MAN WITHOUT A MATE COOKBOOK*. As the title indicates, it's a cookbook written for unmarried men and is organized around our lifestyle. The dishes or meals we need to prepare flow from the events of our lives and the needs of those to be served, whether children, grandchildren, co-workers, a girlfriend or ourselves.

As I spilled and burned my way through the last few years, I discovered a couple of very important things. First, my self-esteem and self-confidence increased immeasurably. It was a major accomplishment to work with my hands and have the dish or meal turn out halfway right. Secondly, even if I botched it completely, the people being served took note of the time and effort I had put forth for them. And that did things to them. In short, it melted their hearts!

So, while this book is a cookbook, it's not the food nor one's cooking skill that is the real issue. While they are important, the essence of it all is what happens when one takes the time and makes the effort to do something for someone else. This cookbook is designed to help you do that for a variety of life situations.

"Whether you think you can or think you can't, you're right."

— Henry Ford

Chapter I

THE BASICS

"Naked rolling pins? Jelly roll pans? Heat to a drizzle consistency? Cream the sugar and shortening?"

"Come on! Give me a break! What is all this? I can't even *read* this miserable book, let alone do what it's talking about! Why isn't there a cookbook for guys like me who are not professional cooks?"

"And all the 'stuff ' I need so I can do what needs doing; my former wife has it all! Where do I start? Pots, pans, casseroles, etc., etc. Big ones? Little ones? Good ones or cheap ones? Who cares? It's going to cost a fortune either way. Why isn't there a cookbook that simply lists the basic things I need?"

"The kids are coming this weekend and I've got this pork loin in the refrigerator. Now what do I do? What goes with it? And what do I do first so everything is done together? This is madness!"

"Why isn't there a cookbook with menus for guys like me who don't want their kids to think their dad is an old poop?"

"This lasagne recipe for my potluck party calls for an 8-ounce carton of ricotta cheese. *Eureka!* Here's the ricotta cheese! Now for an 8-ounce carton. No 8-ounce carton! A 15-ounce carton, but *no* 8-ounce carton. *AAAAgh!*" (Twenty minutes of *AAAAgh's*) "I'll go with the 15-ounce carton! This recipe better be wrong, or my party guests will have ricotta cheese coming out their nostrils! Now for nine lasagne noodles. *AAAAgh!* They don't say how many noodles are in a package! Just pounds! Who cares? I only *need* nine noodles! I thought this was going to be easy! Why isn't there a cookbook with shopping lists to tell us what to buy?"

"Nuts to this! If there isn't one, then write one!"

"I can't do that!" (Five years of "I can't do that!")

"To do that I'm going to have to admit I don't know what I'm doing and ask for help! Can't do that! It's like being lost in a strange neighborhood and having to stop and ask for directions. *Can't do that!*"

But in asking, I received. I received far more than I asked for! Instead of humiliation, I received respect; instead of embarrassment, I received admiration. Instead of marrying a cook, I became one, and a broken family was restored. Instead of being alone, I'm surrounded by loving people of all sorts.

All these benefits from cooking for others? No, but it helped, and serves to illustrate what can happen when one concentrates on serving others. So, get your "stuff " together and just do it!

Basic Cooking Terms

To Prepare

• *Chop*	Cut food into irregular-sized pieces.
• *Crush*	Press with side of knife, mallet or rolling pin to break into small pieces.
• *Cube*	Cut into 1/2-inch or wider strips; cut across into cubes.
• *Cut up*	Cut into small pieces with kitchen scissors.
• *Dice*	Cut into 1/2-inch or narrower strips; cut across into cubes.
• *Flute*	Press a decorative pattern into the raised edge of a pie crust.
• *Grate*	Cut into tiny particles by rubbing food across the small rough holes of a grater.
• *Grease*	Spread bottom and sides of pan with shortening or spray with nonstick cooking spray.
• *Peel*	Remove outer layer of food with a knife, vegetable parer or fingers.
• *Shred*	Cut into long thin pieces by using a shredder, a knife or a food processor fitted with a shredding disc.
• *Slice*	Cut food into same-sized flat pieces.
• *Snip*	Cut into very small pieces with kitchen scissors.

To Combine

• *Beat*	Combine ingredients usually until smooth, by vigorous over-and-over motion with spoon, hand beater, wire whisk or electric mixer.
• *Blend*	Thoroughly combine two or more ingredients by hand, or by using an appliance such as a blender, mixer or food processor.
• *Fold*	Mix gently, bringing rubber scraper down through mixture, across the bottom, up and over top until blended.
• *Mix*	Combine in any way that distributes all ingredients evenly.
• *Stir*	Combine ingredients with a circular or figure eight motion until mixture is of a uniform consistency.
• *Toss*	Mix ingredients lightly with a lifting motion.

To Cook

• *Bake*	Cook in oven.
• *Baste*	Spoon or brush a liquid over food during cooking.
• *Boil*	Heat until bubbles rise continuously and break on the surface of the liquid or mixture.
• *Broil*	Cook under or over a direct heat source.
• *Brown*	Cook on top of the stove over medium heat until surface of food changes color.
• *Cook & stir*	Cook rapidly in small amount of fat, stirring occasionally.
• *Simmer*	Cook in liquid just below boiling point. Bubbles form slowly and collapse below the surface.

BASIC COOKING TERMS, *continued*

WEIGHTS AND MEASURES

• *Dash*	=	Less than 1/8th of a teaspoon
• *1 tablespoon*	=	3 teaspoons
• *4 tablespoons*	=	1/4 cup
• *8 tablespoons*	=	1/2 cup
• *12 tablespoons*	=	3/4 cup
• *16 tablespoons*	=	1 cup
• *1 cup of liquid*	=	1/2 pint
• *2 cups of liquid*	=	1 pint
• *4 cups of liquid*	=	1 quart
• *2 pints of liquid*	=	1 quart
• *4 quarts*	=	1 gallon
• *8 quarts*	=	1 peck
• *16 ounces*	=	1 pound
• *8 fluid ounces*	=	1 cup
• *4 fluid ounces*	=	1/2 cup

*'Serve one
another in love.'*
Gal. 5:13

BASIC EQUIPMENT NEEDS

To prepare the meals and dishes in this cookbook, it's recommended that one's kitchen have the following basic items, in addition to a range with an oven, a microwave and a refrigerator with a freezer.

FOOD PREPARATION

- Mixing bowls (3 or 4 assorted sizes)
- Wooden spoons
- Plastic or metal mixing spoons
- Slotted spoon
- Long-handled fork
- Kitchen scissors
- Rubber spatulas (wide and narrow)
- Cutting board
- Liquid measuring cup (1-cup size)
- Dry measuring cups (a nested set)
  (1/4, 1/3, 1/2 and 1-cup measures)
- Measuring spoons (a set)
  (1/4, 1/2, 1 teaspoon, 1 tablespoon)
- Strainer and/or colander
- Grater or shredder
- Openers–can, bottle and jar
- Pancake turner

- Vegetable parer
- Knives:
  Paring (2- to 3-inch blade)
  Slicing
  Chef or French
  Serrated bread
- Timer
- Pot holders/Oven mits
- Vegetable brush
- Toaster
- Meat thermometer
- Rolling pin
- Tongs
- Wire whisk
- Corkscrew
- Coffeemaker
- Portable or stand electric mixer

COOKING

- Skillets (frying pans) with covers:
  (8-inch, and 10- or 12-inch)
- Saucepans with covers: 1-, 2- and 3-quart
- Dutch oven with cover (heavyweight preferred)

BAKING

- Cookie sheets (without sides)
- Baking pans:
  8x8x2-inch
  9x9x2-inch
  13x9x2-inch
- Round layer pans
  (8x1 1/2 , or 9x1 1/2-inches)

- Loaf pan (9x5x3-inch)
- Jelly roll pan (15 1/2x10 1/2x1-inch)
- Pie plate (9x1 1/4-inches)
- Covered casseroles: 1-, 2- and 3-quart
- Roasting pan with rack
- Round 2- to 3-inch cookie cutter

BASIC EQUIPMENT NEEDS, *continued*

MICROWAVING

- 2-quart microwave-safe bowl with handle and spout
- Bacon rack
- 2-cup microwave-safe measuring cup
- 10x7x1 1/2-inch microwave-safe baking dish
- Paper towels
- Waxed paper

CLEAN-UP

- Dish towels
- Dish cloth or sponge
- Pot scrubber
- Dish drainer
- Paper towels

STORAGE

- Plastic bags (zip-lock type are nice)
- Covered containers (commercial or saved from purchased items)
- Tightly covered jars (saved from purchased items)
- Aluminum foil
- Plastic wrap

MISCELLANEOUS

- Lunch bags
- Paper napkins
- Paper cups and plates
- Plastic forks, knives and spoons

NICE TO HAVE

- Tube pan (10 x 4 inches) or 12-cup bundt pan
- 9-inch springform pan
- Pizza pans
- Cooling racks
- Electric fry pan
- Blender or food processor
- Griddle
- Potato masher
- Pastry cloth
- Stockinette cover for rolling pin
- Pastry blender
- Pastry brushes for basting
- Garlic press
- Grapefruit knife
- Pepper mill
- Salad spinner
- Muffin pans
- Custard cups

STOCKING THE CUPBOARD

Only by experience will one learn which foods are important to keep on hand. The following basic ingredients will be needed not only for the menus and recipes in this cookbook but in many other recipes. Additional supplies, as needed, are listed with each menu.

For each menu, the smallest size package needed for the recipe is listed in the shopping list. It may be more economical to purchase some items in larger sizes if they will be used again soon. Spices and herbs may be available in bulk at some large supermarkets and co-ops, and can be purchased in small amounts for one's immediate needs. These will also be fresher, but need to be stored in small, tightly covered jars.

THE CUPBOARD

- All-purpose flour
- Sugar (granulated, brown, powdered)
- Honey
- Peanut butter
- Baking mix (Bisquick)
- Pancake syrup
- Cornstarch
- Shortening
- Vegetable oil
- Olive oil
- Vinegar (apple cider and white)
- Rice (regular and quick-cooking)
- Baking powder
- Baking soda
- Cream of tartar
- Vanilla extract
- Almond extract
- Instant bouillon or cubes (chicken and beef)
- Worcestershire sauce
- Tabasco sauce
- Light corn syrup
- Dry bread crumbs
- Unsweetened cocoa
- Grated Parmesan cheese
- No-stick cooking spray
- Toothpicks

THE REFRIGERATOR

- Milk
- Butter or margarine
- Eggs
- Mayonnaise type salad dressing
- Head of lettuce
- Catsup and jar of mustard
- Soy sauce
- Lemon juice (bottled)
- Bread
- Garlic (fresh or jar of finely chopped)
- Coffee

SEASONINGS, HERBS AND SPICES

- Salt
- Onion salt
- Garlic salt
- Celery salt
- Black pepper
- Cayenne pepper
- Garlic powder
- Chili powder
- Dried oregano powder
- Paprika
- Celery seed
- Whole allspice
- Dried basil leaves
- Dried oregano leaves
- Dried thyme leaves
- Bay leaves
- Dried tarragon leaves
- Dry mustard
- Ground cinnamon
- Ground ginger
- Ground cloves
- Ground nutmeg

TABLE SETTINGS

BASIC TABLE SETTING

(1)   (2) (3)

For a basic lunch or dinner menu, use a 3-piece place setting: dinner fork (1), dinner knife (2) and teaspoon (3). Arrange them as the diagram illustrates.

TABLE SETTING FOR ENTERTAINING

(1) (2)   (3) (4) (5)

For a more formal lunch or dinner menu, use a 5-piece place setting: salad fork (1), dinner fork (2), dinner knife (3), soup spoon (4) and teaspoon (5). Arrange them as the diagram illustrates. It's appropriate also to use a tablecloth or place mats when entertaining.

"...The chief thing that separates us from God is the thought that we are separated from Him. If we get rid of that thought, our troubles will be greatly reduced...." — Thomas Keating
(*Open Mind, Open Heart*, Element, Inc., 1991, Rockport, MA)

CHAPTER II

MEALS ALONE

Living alone has many features that I have learned to enjoy and appreciate. But meals alone is not one of them! Of all the aspects of the home-alone lifestyle, I find eating alone to be just about the pits. To me the only thing worse is cleaning the bathroom!

Buying groceries for one is almost a bad joke. I eat only a small portion of what I do buy, and the rest becomes the home for all sorts of little creepy creatures. Flour becomes home to little black bugs, and raisins are host to little white worms. Cans ferment and explode from old age, and the refrigerator always has something in it that is ripe and ready for the distillery. My children are forever checking the dates on cartons to see if the contents are safe to eat.

More than a few times have I wondered, "What incredibly stupid thing(s) did I do, or not do, to end up like this? How do I get out of this situation? I 'need' someone to cook for me!"

There appeared to be two options: eat out or get married again.

Eating out all the time gets old in a hurry, not to mention the expense. But I did learn that the *Cheers* lifestyle is for real. My favorite hostess doesn't bother to seat me anymore. She just waves me on with her "My feet hurt" excuse. The waitress brings my "usual" and leaves me ... to eat alone!

"I'm *paying* to eat alone? This is not the right answer!"

In exploring the second option I discovered I would effectively end up with two wives, two sets of children, two budgets and two mothers-in-law.

"Whoa! Too many twos! The responsibility for one of each of the above is enough for me!"

I came to realize that to find someone simply to cook for me (take care of me, generally) was selfishness on my part. Another person can't save me from my predicament. Besides, mates and marriage are not the source of personal security, peace and contentment anyway.

"So, who is?"

Over the years I've learned that I have a loving God who is as close and intimate as I choose to allow Him to be. He is my security. In reality I'm never alone.

So, while my situation hasn't changed, everything is different. I've learned to cook! I've also learned to be content in my present circumstances. Together, we'll turn life's lemons into lemonade!

Hopefully, the menus in this chapter will make eating alone more enjoyable. The servings are ample, tasty and nutritious.

BREAKFAST

Racing Against Time

Nutritious Spread for Toast Blended Morning Shake

MEAL PREPARATION SCHEDULE

Prepare spread; toast bread; prepare shake.

Preparation Time: 10 minutes.

(+) indicates that this is the smallest size available; there will be leftovers.

SHOPPING LIST

- 1 (12-ounce) carton cottage cheese(+)
- 1 orange(+)
- 1 small banana
- 1 (6- or 8-ounce) carton yogurt(+)
- *Check cupboard* for chunky peanut butter, honey and sugar.
- *Check refrigerator* for butter or margarine, bread and milk.

Recipes

NUTRITIOUS SPREAD FOR WHOLE WHEAT TOAST *(2/3 cup)*

> 2 tablespoons chunky peanut butter
> 1 tablespoon honey
> 1/2 cup cottage cheese
> 2 slices whole wheat toast

In small bowl, blend peanut butter, honey and cottage cheese until mixed. Spread on toast.

BLENDED MORNING SHAKE *(1 large serving)*

> 1/2 orange, peeled
> 1/2 cup milk
> 1 small banana, sliced
> 1 tablespoon sugar
> 1/3 cup plain or flavored yogurt

Cut orange half into 4 pieces. Pour milk into blender container; add orange and remaining ingredients. Cover and blend on medium speed until smooth. Pour into glass.

"Better a dry crust with peace and quiet than a house full of feasting, with strife."
Proverbs 17:1 (NIV)

BREAKFAST

Hot Cereal

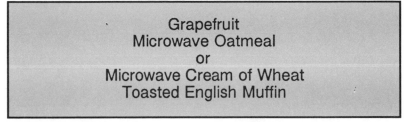

Grapefruit
Microwave Oatmeal
or
Microwave Cream of Wheat
Toasted English Muffin

MEAL PREPARATION SCHEDULE

Section grapefruit; microwave cereal; toast muffin.

Preparation Time: 10 minutes.

(+) indicates that this is the smallest size available; there will be leftovers.

SHOPPING LIST

- 1 grapefruit(+)
- 1 (18-ounce) package quick-cooking rolled oats(+) or
- 1 (28-ounce) package instant Cream of Wheat(+)
- 1 (13-ounce) package English Muffins(+)
- *Check cupboard* for granulated sugar or brown sugar.
- *Check refrigerator* for butter or margarine and milk.

Recipes

GRAPEFRUIT

Cut grapefruit in half. Using serrated knife or grapefruit knife, cut around each section of one half. Cover remaining half with plastic wrap; refrigerate. (This will keep for 2 to 3 days.)

MICROWAVE OATMEAL *(1 serving)*

> 2/3 cup hot tap water
> 1/3 cup quick-cooking rolled oats
> Salt, if desired

In 2-cup microwave-safe bowl, combine water, oats and salt. Microwave on HIGH for 1 1/2 to 2 minutes or until thickened. Stir. Serve with milk and granulated sugar or brown sugar.

MICROWAVE CREAM OF WHEAT *(1 serving)*

> 3/4 cup hot tap water
> 2 1/2 tablespoons instant Cream of Wheat
> Salt, if desired

In 2-cup microwave-safe bowl, combine water, Cream of Wheat and salt. Microwave on HIGH for 1 1/2 to 2 1/2 minutes, or until thickened. Stir. Serve with milk and granulated sugar or brown sugar.

LUNCH

Brown Bag Lunch

> Pocket Bread Sandwich
> Cherry Tomatoes
> Apple
> Cookies

MEAL PREPARATION SCHEDULE

Cookies could be homemade (ahead of time) or purchased. If rushed for time in the morning, wash apple and cherry tomatoes the evening before. Meat for sandwich can be purchased at the deli and chopped ahead, covered and refrigerated.

Preparation Time: 10 to 15 minutes.

(+) indicates that this is the smallest size available; there will be leftovers.

SHOPPING LIST

- 1 package (6-inch) pocket bread(+)
- 2 ounces cooked chicken or ham*
- Alfalfa sprouts*
- Shredded cheese*
- Sunflower seeds (nuts)*
- Cherry tomatoes*
- 1 apple
- Cookies (if not homemade)
- *Check cupboard* for lunch bag and napkins.
- *Check refrigerator* for lettuce and mayonnaise.

---

*Can be bought at a supermarket salad bar if you don't use them often or don't care for a lot of preparation.

Recipe

POCKET BREAD SANDWICH *(1 serving)*

1 (6-inch) pocket bread round
Mayonnaise or salad dressing
2 ounces cooked chicken or ham, chopped
1/4 cup chopped lettuce
2 tablespoons alfalfa sprouts
2 tablespoons shredded cheese
1 tablespoon sunflower seeds

Cut bread round in half crosswise, making 2 pockets. Spread a thin layer of mayonnaise on inside of each pocket. Place half of meat in each pocket; add lettuce, sprouts, cheese and seeds. Wrap in plastic wrap; refrigerate. *(Try different combinations if desired; pineapple is good with ham.)*

LUNCH

Lunch at Home

> Grilled Bacon, Tomato, Cheese Sandwich
> Dill Pickles
> Carrot and Celery Sticks
> Flavored Yogurt

MEAL PREPARATION SCHEDULE

Wash and peel carrots; wash celery stalks. Cut carrots and celery into 3-inch strips. Wash tomato. Cook bacon, slice tomato, assemble and grill sandwich.

Preparation Time: 15 to 20 minutes.

(+) *indicates that this is the smallest size available; there will be leftovers.*

SHOPPING LIST

- 1 (8-ounce) package sliced cheese(+)
- 1 (8-ounce) package sliced bacon(+)
- 1 tomato
- 1 small jar dill pickles
- 1 pound carrots(+)
- 1 bunch celery(+)
- 1 (6- or 8-ounce) carton flavored yogurt
- *Check refrigerator* for butter or margarine and bread.

Recipe

GRILLED BACON, TOMATO, CHEESE SANDWICH *(1 serving)*

> 2 slices bacon
> Butter or margarine
> 2 slices bread
> 1 tomato, cut into 3 or 4 slices
> 1 slice cheese

Place bacon between 2 paper towels on microwave rack or microwave-safe dish. Microwave on HIGH for 2 to 2 1/2 minutes or until crisp. Or, cook in skillet until crisp; drain on paper towels.

Heat griddle or skillet over medium heat. Butter 1 side of each slice of bread. Place 1 slice buttered side down on griddle; top with bacon, tomato and cheese. Place second bread slice on top of cheese, buttered side up. Grill until bottom bread slice is golden brown. Turn sandwich with pancake turner; grill until other side is golden brown and cheese is melted.

"...You will leave me all alone. Yet I am not alone, for my Father is with me."
John 16:32 (NIV)

LUNCH

Thermos Lunch

Hamburger Bean Bake
Fresh Pear
Crusty Roll
Cookies or Bars

MEAL PREPARATION SCHEDULE

The evening before or on a weekend, prepare Hamburger Bean Bake; refrigerate. Wash pear and butter roll, if desired.

Preparation Time: About 30 minutes to prepare; about 1 hour to bake.

SHOPPING LIST

- 1 pound ground beef
- 1 medium onion
- 1 (16-ounce) can pork and beans
- 1 (16-ounce) can kidney beans, drained
- 1 (16-ounce) can butter beans or lima beans
- Fresh pear
- Crusty roll
- Cookies or bars (if not homemade)
- *Check cupboard* for vinegar, brown sugar and salt.
- *Check refrigerator* for butter or margarine, catsup and prepared mustard.

Recipe

HAMBURGER BEAN BAKE *(6 servings)*

1 pound ground beef
1/2 cup chopped onion
1 (16-ounce) can pork and beans
1 (16-ounce) can kidney beans, drained
1 (16-ounce) can butter beans or lima beans, drained
1/2 cup catsup
1 tablespoon vinegar
1 teaspoon prepared mustard
1/2 cup packed brown sugar
1/2 teaspoon salt

Brown ground beef and onion in skillet over medium heat on range or in microwave on HIGH for 5 to 6 minutes, stirring once or twice to break up meat; drain off fat. In 3-quart casserole, combine ground beef and onion with remaining ingredients. Bake covered at 350 degrees for 45 to 60 minutes. Cool slightly; refrigerate. Reheat amount needed to fill wide-mouth thermos in morning. Freeze remaining mixture in individual portions that will fill thermos.

EVENING DINNER

Chicken Fajita

> Chicken Fajita in Tortilla
> Sour Cream or Salsa
> Corn Chips
> Cantaloupe Slice
> Ice Cream

MEAL PREPARATION SCHEDULE

Prepare marinade and meat the night before or at least 2 hours before serving. Slice cantaloupe (if purchased whole or half melon). Fry chicken and vegetables. Warm tortilla.

Preparation Time: 20 to 25 minutes to prepare marinade and chicken; overnight or 2 hours standing time; 5 to 6 minutes to cook.

(+) indicates that this is the smallest size available; there will be leftovers

SHOPPING LIST

- 5 to 6 ounces boneless chicken breast
- 1 small onion
- 1 green bell pepper(+)
- 1 package 10-inch flour tortillas(+)
- 1 (8-ounce) carton dairy sour cream(+)
- 1 (8-ounce) jar salsa(+)
- 1 (10-ounce) package corn chips(+)
- Fresh cantaloupe slice, half or whole melon
- Ice cream
- *Check cupboard* for vegetable oil, salt, garlic powder and chili powder.

Recipe

CHICKEN FAJITA *(1 serving)*

1/2 cup vegetable oil
1/2 teaspoon salt
1/2 teaspoon garlic powder
1 teaspoon chili powder
5 to 6 ounces boneless chicken breast, cut into 3-inch strips
1 small onion, cut into strips
1/2 green bell pepper, cut into strips
Flour tortilla*
1 to 2 tablespoons dairy sour cream
Salsa

The night before or 2 hours before serving, combine vegetable oil, salt, garlic powder and chili powder in glass or plastic container. Add chicken, onion and green pepper; stir to coat chicken and vegetable pieces. Cover and marinate in refrigerator 2 hours or overnight. Remove chicken, onion and green pepper from marinade. In skillet over medium heat, cook chicken and vegetables, stirring constantly until chicken is no longer pink. Warm tortilla in microwave on HIGH about 10 seconds. Serve chicken-vegetable mixture in warm tortilla with sour cream and salsa.
Tip: Extra tortillas can be frozen.

EVENING DINNER

Pork Stir-Fry

> **Stir-Fry Pork with Vegetables**
> **Rice**
> **Orange Slices**
> **Glazed Cake or Shortcake**

Meal Preparation Schedule

The day before, prepare cake. Cool. On day of dinner, prepare cake glaze or topping. Slice orange; place on leaf of lettuce on salad plate. Refrigerate salad until serving time. Slice meat. Prepare rice according to package directions; keep warm. Cook pork and vegetables.

Preparation Time: 20 to 25 minutes just before meal time if cake is baked the day before. Mixing and baking cake, 30 to 45 minutes.

(+) indicates that this is the smallest size available; there will be leftovers.

SHOPPING LIST

- 4 to 5 ounces boneless pork loin
- 1 (16-ounce) package fresh stir-fry vegetables(+) (available in supermarket produce section)
- 1 medium orange
- 1 (1-layer) package yellow cake mix
- 1 (11 1/2-ounce) package milk chocolate chips(+) or 1 fresh peach or 8 to 10 fresh strawberries
- *Check cupboard* for rice, vegetable oil, ground ginger, dry mustard, corn syrup and sugar.
- *Check refrigerator* for lettuce, butter or margarine, soy sauce and eggs.

Recipes

STIR-FRY PORK WITH VEGETABLES *(1 serving)*

1 tablespoon vegetable oil
4 to 5 ounces boneless pork loin, cut into thin 2 x 1/4-inch strips*
Dash ground ginger
Dash dry mustard
1 to 2 cups fresh stir-fry vegetables**
1 tablespoon soy sauce

In medium skillet over medium high heat, heat oil. Add pork strips; stir constantly until brown. Add ginger and mustard; stir. Add vegetables and toss with pork strips. Cover and cook 1 1/2 to 2 minutes until vegetables are crisp-tender. Add soy sauce; cook and stir 1 minute longer.

* Partially freeze pork for ease in cutting.
** 1 (10-ounce) package frozen stir-fry vegetables can be substituted for fresh.

EVENING DINNER

Pork Stir-Fry Menu, continued

CAKE WITH VARIATIONS

1 (1-layer) yellow cake mix
1 egg
Water
Quick Chocolate Glaze or Shortcake Topping (below)

Prepare and bake cake mix according to package directions. Cool; cut into serving size pieces. Freeze unused pieces.

QUICK CHOCOLATE GLAZE

For each serving:
In glass measuring cup, combine 1 tablespoon milk chocolate chips, 2 teaspoons corn syrup and 2 teaspoons margarine. Microwave on MEDIUM (50%) power for 1 minute or until chips are melted; stir. Spread on top of cake.
(Tip: A prepared frozen or bakery cake layer can be substituted for the cake mix, egg and water).

QUICK SHORTCAKE TOPPING

For each serving:
In small bowl, combine 1 fresh peach, sliced or 1/2 cup sliced fresh strawberries with 1 to 2 tablespoons sugar; stir. Spoon over piece of cake.

Stir-Fry Variation

Create your own stir-fry recipes with chicken and/or beef. Record them in the space below.

Chicken	*Beef*
• _____	• _____
• _____	• _____
• _____	• _____

"...And do not call anyone on earth 'father,' for you have one Father, and he is in heaven."
Matthew 23:9 (NIV)

EVENING DINNER

Baked Potato with Toppers

Baked Potato
Italian, Mexican or Ham and Cheese Topper
Tossed Salad
Canned Peaches

MEAL PREPARATION SCHEDULE

Bake potato. Meanwhile, prepare salad and refrigerate until serving time. Prepare Topper of your choice. Open canned peaches and place peach halves in sauce dish.

Preparation Time: 30 to 60 minutes.

SHOPPING LIST

- 1 medium to large white baking potato (russet)
- *Italian Topper:*
  1 pound ground beef
  1 (8-ounce) can tomato sauce
  1 (4-ounce) package shredded mozzarella cheese(+)
- *Mexican Topper:*
  1 pound ground turkey
  1 small onion
  1 green bell pepper(+)
  1 (1 1/4-ounce) package taco seasoning mix(+)

SHOPPING LIST, *continued*

  1 (4-ounce) package shredded Cheddar cheese(+)
- *Ham & Cheese Topper:*
  3 ounces cooked ham (from the deli)
  1 (6-ounce) package shredded Swiss cheese(+)
- Salad greens*
- 1 small tomato
- 1 pound carrots(+)
- 1 (8-ounce) bottle salad dressing of your choice(+)
- 1 (8-ounce) can peach halves or slices
- *Check cupboard* for onion salt, dried basil leaves, dried oregano leaves, garlic powder, flour, salt and dry mustard.
- *Check refrigerator* for butter or margarine and milk.

(+) *indicates that this is the smallest size available; there will be leftovers.*

—————

* Can be bought at supermarket salad bar, if using greens other than lettuce.

Recipes

TOSSED SALAD

1 cup salad greens (head lettuce, spinach, romaine or bibb lettuce), washed, dried and torn into bite-size pieces
1 small tomato, cut into wedges
1 carrot, sliced
Bottled salad dressing

In large bowl, toss all greens, tomato and carrot. Serve with dressing.

EVENING DINNER

Baked Potato Menu, continued

BAKED POTATO

1 medium to large white baking potato (russet)
Topper of your choice (below)

Scrub potato with vegetable brush. Prick potato with fork to allow steam to escape. Bake until potato is easily pierced with a fork, 1 to 1 1/4 hours at 375 degrees or place on paper towel not directly in center of microwave; microwave on HIGH for 3 to 4 minutes. Remove from microwave and wrap in foil or towel to keep heat in and to finish cooking. *(Skin of microwaved potato will not be as crisp as oven-baked potato.)*

Cut criss-cross gash in top; squeeze gently until some of potato pops up through opening. Serve with one of the Toppers below.

ITALIAN TOPPER

1 pound ground beef
1 (8-ounce) can tomato sauce
1/2 teaspoon onion salt
1/2 teaspoon dried basil leaves
1/4 teaspoon dried oregano leaves
Dash garlic powder
2 ounces (1/2 cup) shredded mozzarella cheese

Brown ground beef in skillet over medium heat on range, or in microwave on HIGH for 5 to 6 minutes, stirring two or three times to break up meat; drain off fat. Stir in tomato sauce and seasonings. Cook about 5 minutes over low heat, stirring occasionally, or in microwave until heated. Divide mixture into thirds. Serve 1 portion over hot baked potato and top with cheese; freeze 2 portions in small containers for use later.

MEXICAN TOPPER

1 pound ground turkey
1 small onion, chopped
1/2 green bell pepper, chopped
1/2 (1 1/4-ounce) package taco seasoning mix
1/3 cup water
2 ounces (1/2 cup) shredded Cheddar cheese

Brown ground turkey, onion and green pepper in skillet over medium heat. Drain fat if necessary. Stir in taco seasoning and water. Cook over low heat for about 5 minutes, stirring occasionally. Divide mixture into thirds. Serve 1 portion over hot baked potato and top with cheese; freeze 2 portions in small containers for use later.

(continued, next page)

EVENING DINNER

Baked Potato Menu, continued

HAM & CHEESE TOPPER

1 tablespoon butter or margarine
1 tablespoon flour
Dash salt
1/2 cup milk
1/8 teaspoon dry mustard
1 1/2 ounces (1/3 cup) shredded Swiss cheese
1/2 cup cubed cooked ham

In medium microwave-safe bowl, melt butter in microwave on HIGH for 15 to 20 seconds. Stir in flour and salt; blend to smooth paste. Add milk, stirring constantly. Microwave on HIGH for 2 minutes, stirring twice until mixture thickens. Stir in mustard and cheese. Add ham and microwave on HIGH for 60 to 90 seconds until mixture is hot. Spoon over hot baked potato.

*'The Lord is close
to the brokenhearted.'*
Psalm 34:18

EVENING DINNER

Shrimp Rice Fluff

Shrimp Rice Fluff
Corn Bread Sticks
Fresh Plums

MEAL PREPARATION SCHEDULE

Bake corn bread sticks as directed on package. Wash pepper; cut in half and remove seeds. Prepare Shrimp Rice Fluff. Wash plums.

Preparation Time: 15 minutes; 5 minutes standing time.

SHOPPING LIST

- 1 (6-ounce) package frozen cooked shrimp or 1 (4 1/4-ounce) can shrimp
- 1 small onion
- 1 (8-ounce) can tomato sauce
- 2-ounces fresh pea pods
- 1 small red bell pepper
- 1 (7-ounce) package refrigerated corn sticks or bakery corn bread sticks
- Fresh plums or other fresh fruit
- *Check cupboard* for chicken bouillon cube, cayenne pepper and quick-cooking rice.
- *Check refrigerator* for butter or margarine and garlic clove.

Recipe

SHRIMP RICE FLUFF *(1 large serving)*

1 (6-ounce) package frozen cooked shrimp
    or 1 (4 1/4-ounce) can shrimp
1 tablespoon margarine or butter
1/4 cup chopped onion
1 clove garlic, finely chopped
3/4 cup water
1 chicken bouillon cube
1 (8-ounce) can tomato sauce
1/4 teaspoon cayenne pepper
2 ounces (1/2 cup) fresh pea pods
1 small red bell pepper, sliced
3/4 cup quick-cooking rice

Rinse shrimp in cold water; drain and set aside. In skillet over medium heat, melt margarine. Stir in onion and garlic; cook until onion is tender. Add water, bouillon cube, tomato sauce, cayenne pepper and shrimp; heat to boiling. Stir in pea pods, red pepper and rice. Cover; remove from heat and let stand 5 minutes. Fluff with a fork.

"...He will turn the hearts of the fathers to their children, and the hearts of the children to their fathers...." — Malachi 4:6 (NIV)

CHAPTER III

WEEKENDS WITH THE KIDS

The change from a married-with-family lifestyle to a weekends-with-the-kids lifestyle was a shock. The adjustment was hard, unpleasant and unwanted. It took a lot of getting-used-to-it, to get used to it.

My self-confidence and self-esteem were in shambles. My sense of identity was utterly gone. "Who am I?" "What am I?" "What do I do?" On the inside I felt like the scrawny ninety-pound weakling on the beach!

From this experience I learned that much of life is what we choose to make of it. Regardless of the lifestyle of others, I was morally responsible to God for my own actions and decisions. Given what I had to deal with, what was the right way to deal with it?

There were two major concerns facing me. First and foremost, my children needed to know they were loved. The breakup of my marriage was not their doing, not their fault, not their responsibility. While they were innocently caught in the wake of this turbulence, they still were loved and accepted. Children can do without a lot, but they cannot live without the acceptance and approval of a loving father.

The second area of concern followed from the first. We needed a home, a place of stability, security and safety. Living out of the back seat of "Herbie" or with a friend wouldn't do. Even though I was alone, it was important to establish a place the kids knew they could come to anytime, dump their stuff and take off again to visit friends and family.

Instead of having weekends with the kids, we were together during the summer months and every other holiday. It worked well. We had big blocks of uninterrupted time with each other. It was quality, not quantity, that counted the most.

It was during these times that we suffered through many meals that were not quite what they were intended to be. However, they served as expressions of love, and aided in establishing a home. Hopefully, the following menus will assist others in doing the same.

BREAKFAST

Pancakes and Sausage

> Orange Juice
> Pancakes
> Oven Sausage

MEAL PREPARATION SCHEDULE

The night before, place frozen juice can in refrigerator to thaw. In the morning, prepare the juice. Heat oven to 375 degrees; measure ingredients for pancakes; place sausage in oven: make pancakes.

Preparation Time: 25 minutes.

SHOPPING LIST

- 1 (12-ounce) can frozen orange juice concentrate
- 1 (12-ounce) package link sausages
- *Check cupboard* for vegetable oil, flour, sugar, baking powder, salt and syrup.
- *Check refrigerator* for butter or margarine, eggs and milk.

Recipes

ORANGE JUICE

Pour juice concentrate into pitcher; add water following directions on can. Stir and refrigerate until serving time.

PANCAKES *(12 [4-inch] pancakes)*

> 2 eggs
> 1 1/2 cups milk
> 3 tablespoons vegetable oil
> 1 3/4 cups flour
> 1 tablespoon sugar
> 3 teaspoons baking powder
> 3/4 teaspoon salt

Break eggs into large mixing bowl; beat with fork. Add milk and oil to eggs; stir well. Heat skillet or griddle over medium-high heat (380 degrees for electric fry pan). Measure and combine dry ingredients; add to egg mixture. Stir until dry ingredients are well moistened (a few lumps will remain). Lightly grease skillet. Pour about 1/3 cup of batter into skillet for each pancake. Flip pancakes after bubbles appear on surface and pancakes look dry on edges. Flip only once. Cook until golden. Pour 1 cup syrup into a microwave-safe container and heat on HIGH for 90 seconds. Serve with margarine or butter and syrup.

OVEN SAUSAGE

Allow 2 sausages per person. Heat oven to 375 degrees. Place sausages in pie plate or cake pan. Bake 10 minutes. Turn sausages with tongs; bake 10 minutes longer or until golden brown. Remove pan from oven; remove sausages from pan and drain on paper towels.

BREAKFAST

Old-Fashioned French Toast

> French Toast
> Strawberries and Powdered Sugar
> Cocoa

MEAL PREPARATION SCHEDULE

The cocoa mix recipe is enough for about 50 servings. Make anytime and store in tightly covered container. The night before, place frozen strawberries in refrigerator to thaw. In the morning, prepare French Toast; heat water for Cocoa.

Preparation Time: 15 minutes.

(+) indicates that this is the smallest size available; there will be leftovers.

SHOPPING LIST

- 1 loaf white, cinnamon or French bread(+)
- 1 (8-quart) package instant nonfat dry milk
- 1 (16-ounce) package instant cocoa mix
- 1 (6-ounce) jar non-dairy powdered creamer
- 1 (10-ounce) package frozen strawberries
- *Check cupboard* for powdered sugar.
- *Check refrigerator* for eggs and milk.

Recipes

FRENCH TOAST *(8 slices)*

2 eggs
1/2 cup milk
8 slices bread
1 (10-ounce) package frozen strawberries, thawed
Powdered sugar

Heat skillet over medium heat (360 degrees for electric fry pan). Break eggs into shallow dish or pie plate. Beat eggs with fork. Add milk and mix well. Lightly grease skillet. Dip bread slices into egg mixture, turning to coat both sides. Cook in pan until golden brown; flip and cook other side until golden brown. Serve with strawberries and powdered sugar.

COCOA MIX *(50 servings)*

1 (8-quart) package instant nonfat dry milk
1 (16-ounce) package instant cocoa mix
1 (6-ounce) jar non-dairy powdered creamer
1 cup powdered sugar

Combine all ingredients in large container (a 5-quart plastic ice cream bucket works well). Mix with wooden spoon until well blended. Store tightly covered.
To make 1 serving: Heat 1 cup water to boiling. Place 1/4 cup cocoa mix in drinking cup; add boiling water and stir.

LUNCH

Tuna Cheese Melts

Tuna Cheese Melts
Red or Green Grapes
Peanut Butter-Chocolate Chip Cookies
Milk

MEAL PREPARATION SCHEDULE

Cookies can be prepared ahead of time. Toast bread; prepare tuna mixture; add cheese. While cheese is melting, wash grapes and pour milk.

Preparation Time: 15 minutes (not including cookies). Cookies take 50 to 60 minutes.

SHOPPING LIST

- 1 (6 1/2-ounce) can tuna
- 1 (8-ounce) package sliced American cheese
- 1 (6-ounce) package chocolate chips
- 1 pound grapes
- *Check cupboard* for onion salt, peanut butter, sugar, brown sugar, flour and baking soda.
- *Check refrigerator* for milk, butter or margarine, bread, mayonnaise and eggs.

Recipes

TUNA CHEESE MELTS *(6 open-faced sandwiches)*

1 (6 1/2-ounce) can tuna, well drained
1/4 teaspoon onion salt
3 tablespoons mayonnaise or salad dressing
6 slices bread, toasted
6 slices American cheese

Combine tuna, onion salt and mayonnaise in small bowl. Spread mixture on toast. Top each slice with 1 slice cheese. Place on broiler pan. Broil 2 to 3 minutes or until cheese melts. Sandwiches can also be heated in microwave on MEDIUM (50% power) for 90 seconds or until cheese melts.

PEANUT BUTTER-CHOCOLATE CHIP COOKIES *(5 to 6 dozen)*

1 cup margarine, softened
1 cup crunchy peanut butter
3/4 cup granulated sugar
1 cup packed brown sugar

2 eggs
2 cups all-purpose flour
1 teaspoon baking soda
1 (6-ounce) package chocolate chips

Heat oven to 350 degrees. In large bowl, combine margarine and peanut butter with electric mixer or by hand. Gradually add granulated and brown sugars; blend well. Break eggs into small bowl and beat with a fork. Add eggs to sugar mixture; beat until smooth. Stir in flour and soda. Stir in chocolate chips. Using a teaspoon, drop cookie dough onto ungreased cookie sheet. Slightly flatten cookies with the back of the spoon. Bake 10 to 12 minutes or until golden brown. Remove cookies from cookie sheet with pancake turner. Place on wire racks or waxed paper to cool.

LUNCH

This is an excellent meal where Dad and the kids can cook together. Dad can cut the bread into 1-inch slices and make the fondue while the kids can cut or tear the bread slices into quarters.

Cheese Fondue

Cheese Fondue with French Bread
Broccoli Bites
Apple Slices
Milk

MEAL PREPARATION SCHEDULE

Cut bread. Wash broccoli and apples. Cut apples into slices, break broccoli into bite-size pieces; place on serving plate. Prepare Cheese Fondue.

Preparation Time: 20 minutes.

(+) *indicates that this is the smallest size available; there will be leftovers.*

SHOPPING LIST

- 1 (8-ounce) jar Cheese Whiz
- 1 loaf French bread(+)
- 1 small bunch fresh broccoli
- 2 apples
- *Check cupboard* for flour and dry mustard.
- *Check refrigerator* for butter or margarine and milk.

Recipe

CHEESE FONDUE *(4 servings*)*

2 tablespoons margarine
2 tablespoons flour
1 cup milk
8-ounce jar Cheese Whiz*
1/4 teaspoon dry mustard
1/2 loaf French bread*

In 2-quart microwave-safe bowl, heat margarine on HIGH for 30 seconds or until melted. Stir in flour. Slowly stir in milk. Stir in Cheese Whiz and dry mustard until well blended. Microwave on HIGH for 3 minutes, stirring after each minute. Sauce should be thickening. If sauce is still thin, microwave for 1 minute longer. To serve, place cut-up bread on plate and using fondue fork or regular fork, dip bread into cheese fondue.

---

*Remaining French bread can be used for French toast or sandwiches. Leftover cheese can be refrigerated, reheated in microwave and served with cauliflower or other vegetables.

AFTERNOON SNACKS

It goes without saying that children are always hungry and welcome snacks between meals or in the evenings. In addition to the Cereal Snack Mix (page 48), Fast and Easy Pizza (page 108) and Almost Orange Julius (page 71), the following easy-to-serve snacks are suggested.

QUICKY NACHOS

Tortilla chips
1 (4-ounce) package (1 cup) shredded Cheddar cheese

Spread some chips on a microwave-safe dinner plate. Sprinkle with shredded cheese. Microwave on HIGH for 20 seconds or until cheese is melted; serve warm. Repeat as needed.

CALIFORNIA DIP 'N' CHIPS

2 cups dairy sour cream
1 envelope dry onion soup
Potato chips or chilled cut-up vegetables

Blend sour cream and dry onion soup; cover and refrigerate. Serve with potato chips or chilled cut-up vegetables.

CHILLED VEGGIE STICKS

Carrots
Celery
Peanut butter

Wash and cut up celery; peel carrots and cut up. Store in refrigerator in covered container, covered with cold water. Serve with peanut butter.

APPLE WEDGES WITH CREAM CHEESE SPREAD

1 (8-ounce) package light cream cheese, softened
1/3 cup packed brown sugar
1/2 teaspoon vanilla
1/2 to 1 cup salted peanuts, chopped
Apples, washed

Blend all ingredients except apples. Store covered in refrigerator. Serve as a spread for apple wedges.

AFTERNOON SNACKS

In addition to the snack suggestions, simply having a well-stocked pantry, refrigerator and freezer are helpful for unexpected spur-of-the-moment snacks and quick meals.

THE CUPBOARD

1 or 2 boxes of favorite dry cereals
Canned soups *(chicken noodle, tomato)*
Packaged macaroni and cheese dinner mix
Canned pasta products
Peanut butter
Jelly
Popcorn *(ready-to-eat or microwave)*

Canned fruits *(peaches, pears, etc.)*
Packaged cookies
Graham or cinnamon graham crackers
Ritz crackers
Saltine crackers
Potato chips
Pretzels
Instant pudding mix

THE REFRIGERATOR

Bread/hot dog buns
English muffins
Milk
Fresh fruit in season
Cheese slices
String cheese

Cheese curds
Yogurt
Luncheon meats
Hot dogs
Sodas
Juice or drink boxes *(100% juice)*

THE FREEZER

Frozen pizza *(microwave or regular)*
Microwaveable main dishes
Orange juice concentrate

Ice cream/Ice cream bars
Popsicles

"Children's children are a crown to the aged, and parents are the pride of their children."
Proverbs 17:6 (NIV)

EVENING DINNER

Taco Bake

```
Taco Bake
Mixed Vegetables
Ice Cream Jello
Milk
```

MEAL PREPARATION SCHEDULE

Ice Cream Jello can be made earlier in the day or up to 30 minutes before serving time. Prepare Taco Bake; during last 5 to 10 minutes of baking time, cook vegetables as directed on package.

Preparation Time: Taco Bake takes about 20 minutes to prepare and 15 to 20 minutes to bake; Ice Cream Jello takes about 10 minutes to prepare and needs to chill at least 30 minutes; Vegetables take about 15 minutes.

(+) indicates that this is the smallest size available; there will be leftovers.

SHOPPING LIST

- 1 (4-ounce) can refrigerated crescent dinner rolls
- 1/2 pound ground beef
- 1 (1 1/4-ounce) envelope taco seasoning mix(+)
- 1 (8-ounce) carton dairy sour cream(+)
- 1 (4-ounce) package shredded Cheddar cheese
- 1 small head of lettuce(+)
- 1 large or 2 small tomatoes
- 1 (9-ounce) package frozen mixed vegetables
- 1 (3-ounce) package any flavored gelatin
- 1 pint vanilla ice cream(+)
- *Check refrigerator* for milk.

Recipes

TACO BAKE *(3 to 4 servings)*

1 (4-ounce) can refrigerated crescent dinner rolls
1/2 pound ground beef
1/2 package taco seasoning mix
1/2 cup dairy sour cream
1 (4-ounce) package (1 cup) shredded Cheddar cheese
1 to 2 cups chopped lettuce
1 large or 2 small tomatoes, chopped

Crust: Heat oven to 375 degrees. Grease 9-inch square pan or 9-inch pie plate. Unroll dough carefully; do not separate into triangles. Press seams together so dough is one piece. Place dough in pan. If using round pan, push dough to fit pan. Bake about 5 minutes. Remove from oven.

Filling: Brown ground beef in skillet over medium heat on range or in microwave on HIGH for 4 minutes, stirring once or twice to break up meat. Drain off fat. Add taco seasoning to ground beef; stir well. Cook for about 5 minutes over low heat. Spread meat evenly over partially baked crust in pan. Spread sour cream over meat. Sprinkle with shredded cheese. Bake 15 to 20 minutes or until crust is browned and cheese is melted. While dish is baking, wash lettuce; drain well. Wash tomatoes. Chop lettuce and tomatoes. Remove Taco Bake from oven; top with lettuce and tomatoes. Cut into serving-size pieces.

EVENING DINNER

Taco Bake Menu, continued

ICE CREAM JELLO *(4 servings)*

1 cup water
1 (3-ounce) package flavored gelatin
1 heaping cup vanilla ice cream

Heat water to boiling in saucepan or in microwave. Place gelatin in bowl. Add boiling water; stir until gelatin is dissolved. Add ice cream; stir until melted. Pour into 4 individual serving dishes. Refrigerate until set. (*If you are in a hurry this can be frozen, but make sure the bowls can stand the freezing temperatures.*)

"He will turn the hearts of fathers to their children."
Mal. 4:16

EVENING DINNER

Pizza Casserole

> **Pizza Casserole**
> Bread Sticks
> Tossed Salad with Dressing
> Pudding-Cookie Dessert
> Milk

MEAL PREPARATION SCHEDULE

Pizza Casserole is put together ahead of time and should be refrigerated for at least 3 hours. Pudding-Cookie Dessert can also be made ahead of time. Prepare Tossed Salad during last 10 minutes of casserole baking time.

Preparation Time: Pizza Casserole takes about 10 minutes to prepare; needs to be refrigerated at least 3 hours; baking and standing time: 1 hour, 15 minutes. Salad takes 10 minutes to prepare. Pudding-Cookie Dessert takes 15 minutes to prepare.

SHOPPING LIST

- 1/2 pound ground beef
- 1 (10-ounce) package egg noodles(+)
- 1 (15-ounce) can tomato sauce
- 1 (4-ounce) package shredded mozzarella cheese

SHOPPING LIST, *continued*

- 1 head lettuce, 1 bunch of other greens or a combination (see recipe)
- 2 to 3 tomatoes
- 1 pound carrots(+) or 1 cucumber
- 1 (6-ounce) package salad croutons(+)
- 1 (8-ounce) bottle salad dressing of your choice
- 1 package bread sticks (or from bakery)
- 1 (3 1/2-ounce) package vanilla instant pudding mix
- 1 (8-ounce) container frozen non-dairy whipped topping
- 1 (11 1/2-ounce) package chocolate fudge-striped cookies(+)
- 2 to 3 bananas
- *Check cupboard* for dried basil leaves, dried oregano powder, sugar and salt.
- *Check refrigerator* for milk.

(+) indicates that this is the smallest size available; there will be leftovers.

Recipes

PIZZA CASSEROLE *(4 servings)*

1/2 pound ground beef
2 cups uncooked egg noodles
1 teaspoon dried basil leaves
1/2 teaspoon dried oregano powder
1 teaspoon sugar
1/2 teaspoon garlic salt
3/4 cup milk
1 (15-ounce) can tomato sauce
1 (4-ounce) package (1 cup) shredded mozzarella cheese

EVENING DINNER

Pizza Casserole Menu, continued

Brown ground beef in skillet over medium heat on top of range or in microwave on HIGH for 4 minutes, stirring once or twice to break up meat; drain off fat. Grease 2-quart casserole. In casserole, combine all ingredients, including uncooked noodles. Cover with casserole lid or aluminum foil. Refrigerate at least 3 hours. Remove cover. Bake at 350 degrees for 1 hour or until noodles are tender. Let stand 10 minutes before serving.

TOSSED SALAD *(4 servings)*

3 to 4 cups salad greens
   (iceberg lettuce, spinach, romaine, bibb lettuce)
2 to 3 tomatoes
1 carrot or cucumber
1/4 cup croutons
Bottled salad dressing

Wash lettuce; dry thoroughly using paper towels, clean dish towel or salad spinner. Tear lettuce into bite-size pieces. Wash tomatoes; cut into wedges. Wash carrot; peel and slice or wash and slice cucumber. In large bowl, toss all ingredients except dressing. Serve with dressing.

PUDDING-COOKIE DESSERT *(4 servings)*

1 (3 1/2-ounce) package vanilla instant pudding mix
1 cup milk
1 (8-ounce) container frozen non-dairy whipped topping, thawed
1/2 (11 1/2-ounce) package chocolate fudge-striped cookies
2 to 3 bananas, sliced

In large bowl, combine pudding mix with milk using a wire whisk; mix until well blended. Fold in whipped topping. Break cookies into quarters. Stir cookies and bananas into pudding mix. Spoon into individual dishes or refrigerate in large bowl until serving time.

*"...Sons are a heritage from the Lord,
children a reward from him.
Like arrows in the hands of a warrior
are sons born in one's youth.
Blessed is the man whose quiver is full of them...."*
Psalm 127:3-5 (NIV)

PICNIC

Roll-Up Sandwiches

Roll-Up Sandwiches
Fresh Fruit in Season
Muffin or Buns
Cereal Bar
Lemonade

MEAL PREPARATION SCHEDULE

At least 45 minutes before picnic, prepare Cereal Bars. Wash and dry fruit. In nonmetal container, prepare lemonade according to directions on can; chill. Pack muffins or buns. Prepare Roll-Up Sandwiches.

Preparation Time: Roll-Up Sandwiches take about 15 minutes; Cereal Bars take about 15 minutes, plus time to cool. Lemonade and fruit take about 10 minutes.

Remember to take along napkins, cups, a tablecloth and a cloth to clean hands or wipe up spills.

SHOPPING LIST

- 1 (8-ounce) package bologna
- 1 (8-ounce) piece Cheddar or colby cheese
- Fresh fruit of choice
- 1 (10-ounce) package marshmallows
- 1 (10-ounce) package Rice Krispies(+)
- Muffins or buns (bakery)
- 1 (12-ounce) can frozen lemonade concentrate
- *Check cupboard* for toothpicks.
- *Check refrigerator* for lettuce, butter or margarine.

(+) *indicates that this is the smallest size available; there will be leftovers.*

Recipes

ROLL-UP SANDWICHES *(2 per person)*

For each Roll-Up:
   1 large or 2 small lettuce leaves
   1 slice bologna
   3x1x1-inch piece Cheddar or colby cheese

Wash lettuce; pat dry. Wrap bologna around cheese; wrap lettuce around bologna. Fasten with wooden toothpicks.

CEREAL BARS *(24 bars)*

   1/4 cup margarine or butter
   1 (10-ounce) package marshmallows
   5 3/4 cups Rice Krispies

Grease 13x9x2-inch pan or lightly spray with no-stick cooking spray. Melt margarine in large saucepan over low heat. With wooden spoon, stir in marshmallows until melted. (Fresh marshmallows work best.) Remove saucepan from heat. Stir in cereal until well mixed. Place mixture in greased pan; using waxed paper, press mixture evenly into pan. Cool. Cut into 2x2-inch squares.

*Checklist for Fathers**

If Your Children Were Small Again, What Would You Do Differently?

- *I would be more free to let my children see that I love their mother.*
  A child whose parents love each other has a security and stability about life that is gained in no other way.

- *I would listen more.*
  The father who listens when his child is small will have a child who cares what his father says later in life.

- *I would seek more opportunities to give my child a feeling of belonging.*
  When a child feels he belongs in his family and is of real worth, it is not a big step to also feel accepted, loved and worth something to others and to God.

- *I would express words of appreciation and praise more.*
  Probably no other thing encourages a child to love life, to seek accomplishment, and to gain confidence more than proper, sincere praise–not flattery, but honest compliments when he does well.

- *I would spend more time with them.*

- *I would laugh more.*

...life is largely made up of little things. A father's faithfulness in the small things determines the happiness of his children...

* John M. Drescher, *Checklist for Fathers*, American Tract Society, Garland, TX (Used by permission)

BIRTHDAY PARTY

Birthday Party with Child's Friends
(Elementary School-Aged Children)

When entertaining four or five children, it's helpful to have a theme. For example, an animal theme where everyone brings a favorite stuffed animal and the birthday cake is a teddy bear. Or the theme could be a treasure hunt with clues hidden in the neighborhood or park. The treasure could be an inexpensive compass or magnifying glass or foil-wrapped candy or pennies. Have at least one gift per child; it works best if the prizes are all the same. The cake could be shaped like a magnifying glass (made with one round layer for the lens and one square layer cut in half and joined together to make the handle).

Entertainment ideas can range from renting a video (kids may not sit still long), attending a movie, bumper bowling,* animal tracking at a nature center,* playing at a playground not in your neighborhood, roller or ice skating,* visiting a museum (children's, science or planetarium),* making your own pizza at the local pizza place* or simply playing party games such as pin-the-tail-on-the-donkey or musical chairs.

With such parties it's okay to serve only ice cream and cake. Invite the number of children you are comfortable in handling, have room for, can transport easily or can afford. However, if you do serve a meal, keep it simple.
   * *Reservations are usually required at these places. Also, check operating times.*

Sloppy Joes

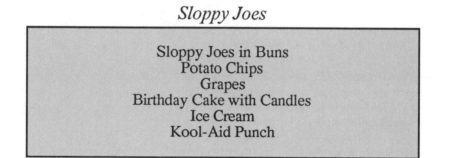

Sloppy Joes in Buns
Potato Chips
Grapes
Birthday Cake with Candles
Ice Cream
Kool-Aid Punch

MEAL PREPARATION SCHEDULE

The day before party, bake cake and cool. If you have time, frost and decorate cake or do early the day of party. Prepare punch early the day of the party; chill. Prepare Sloppy Joes and reheat at serving time. Wash grapes and break into small bunches. Place chips in papernapkin-lined basket. If you have freezer room, make scoops of ice cream ahead of time; place in waxed-paper-lined pan, freeze and bring out at serving time.

Preparation Time: Sloppy Joes take 20 minutes to prepare and 15 minutes to cook; Easy Punch, 10 minutes to prepare; chill several hours; Grapes, 5 minutes; Ice Cream, 10 minutes to scoop; Cake, 10 minutes to prepare. Bake according to package directions; 20 to 25 minutes to frost and decorate.

SHOPPING LIST

- 1-1/2 pounds ground beef
- 1 (8-ounce) can tomato sauce
- 1 dozen hamburger buns
- 1 (8-ounce) box potato chips
- 1 pound seedless grapes
- 2 (2-quart) packages any flavor unsweetened Kool-Aid
- 1 (46-ounce) can pineapple juice
- 1 (2-liter bottle) 7-Up
- 1 (2-layer) package any flavor cake mix
- 1 can any flavor ready-to-spread frosting
- Birthday candles for cake
- 1/2 gallon any flavor ice cream
- Cake Decorations: Tubes of decorator frosting, colored sprinkles, small candies or bear-shaped cookies.
- *Check cupboard* for celery seed, onion salt, sugar and vegetable oil.
- *Check refrigerator* for catsup and eggs.

BIRTHDAY PARTY

Birthday Party with Child's Friends, continued

Recipes

SLOPPY JOES *(8 servings)*

1 1/2 pounds ground beef
3/4 cup catsup
1 (8-ounce) can tomato sauce
1 teaspoon celery seed
1 teaspoon onion salt
1 tablespoon sugar
1 dozen hamburger buns or 18 dollar-size buns

Brown ground beef in skillet, stirring to break meat into small pieces; drain off fat. Add remaining ingredients (except buns) and heat to boiling; reduce heat and simmer about 15 minutes. Serve immediately or refrigerate until just before serving time. Reheat in skillet, stirring occasionally or in covered microwave-safe container for 3 to 4 minutes on HIGH; stir. Spoon into buns and serve.

EASY PUNCH *(About 36 [4-oz.] servings)*

2 (2-quart) packages unsweetened Kool-Aid
1 3/4 cups sugar
8 cups water
1 (46-ounce) can pineapple juice
1 (2-liter) bottle 7-Up, chilled

In nonmetal container, combine Kool-Aid and sugar. Gradually add water, stirring with wooden spoon. Add pineapple juice; mix well. Refrigerate. Add 7-Up just before serving. Serve over ice.

BIRTHDAY CAKE *(12 to 15 servings)*

1 (2-layer) package cake mix
Eggs
Vegetable oil
Water
1 can ready-to-spread frosting
Cake decorations
Birthday candles

Bake cake, following package directions, in 2 layers or 13x9x2-inch pan. Cool; frost as desired. Let the birthday child help decorate the cake.

BIRTHDAY PARTY

Birthday Party for Family at Home

Spaghetti with Meatballs
French Bread
Fruited Gelatin Salad
Birthday Cake
Ice Cream Sundaes
With Homemade Caramel Sauce

MEAL PREPARATION SCHEDULE

The day before, or early the day of the party, bake cake and make gelatin salad. After cake has cooled, frost and decorate. Remember to add fruit cocktail to gelatin. Prepare caramel sauce early and reheat at serving time. Slice and butter bread. Wrap in foil if it is to be heated or put in plastic bag if it is to be served at room temperature. About 45 to 50 minutes before dinner, start to make and bake meatballs. Heat water for spaghetti; cook according to package directions. Add meatballs to spaghetti sauce and heat according to container directions. Heat bread for 10 to 15 minutes, if desired. Remember salad in refrigerator. At dessert time, reheat caramel sauce in microwave, dish up ice cream, light candles on cake.

Preparation Time: Spaghetti takes 20 minutes to prepare. Meatballs take 15 minutes to prepare and 20 to 25 minutes to bake; allow about 10 minutes to heat sauce and meatballs together. French bread about 15 minutes. Gelatin about 10 minutes to prepare. Caramel sauce about 10 minutes to prepare. Birthday cake about 10 minutes to prepare; allow baking time per package directions, 20 to 25 minutes to frost and decorate cake.

SHOPPING LIST

- 1 pound ground beef
- 1 (16-ounce) package spaghetti(+)
- 1 (30-ounce) jar spaghetti sauce without meat
- 1 loaf French bread
- 1 (3-ounce) package gelatin (any flavor)
- 1 (16-ounce) can fruit cocktail
- 1 (2-layer) package any flavor cake mix
- 1 can any flavor ready-to-spread frosting
- Birthday candles
- Cake decorations
- 1/2 gallon any flavor ice cream
- *Check cupboard* for bread crumbs, salt, pepper, dried oregano leaves, dried basil leaves, grated Parmesan cheese, brown sugar, flour and corn syrup.
- *Check refrigerator* for butter or margarine, milk and eggs.

(+) indicates that this is the smallest size available; there will be leftovers.

Recipes

SPAGHETTI *(4 servings)*

1/2 (16-ounce) package

Cook spaghetti according to package directions.

BIRTHDAY PARTY

Birthday Party for Family at Home, continued

MEATBALLS IN SPAGHETTI SAUCE *(5 to 6 servings)*

1 pound ground beef
1 cup dry bread crumbs
1/2 cup milk
1 egg
1 teaspoon salt
1/2 teaspoon dried oregano leaves
1/2 teaspoon dried basil leaves
Dash of pepper
1 (30-ounce) jar spaghetti sauce without meat

Combine all ingredients, except sauce, in medium bowl; mix well. Form into balls. Place on 15 1/2x10x1-inch baking pan. Bake at 375 degrees for 20 to 25 minutes; drain off fat. Add meatballs to spaghetti sauce and heat through. Combine meatballs and sauce with spaghetti and serve with Parmesan cheese, if desired.

FRUITED GELATIN SALAD *(4 to 6 servings)*

1 (3-ounce) package gelatin (any flavor)
1 cup boiling water
1 cup cold water
1 (16-ounce) can fruit cocktail, drained

Place gelatin in bowl. Add boiling water. Stir until gelatin is dissolved, about 1 1/2 to 2 minutes. Add cold water and stir. Refrigerate until partially set. Stir in fruit cocktail. Refrigerate until serving time.

BIRTHDAY CAKE

Use package mix and follow the directions. See page 36 for cake decorating ideas.

CARAMEL SAUCE *(1 1/4 cups)*

1 cup packed brown sugar
1 1/2 tablespoons flour
1/4 cup milk
2 tablespoons corn syrup
3 tablespoons margarine

In 2-quart microwave-safe bowl, mix brown sugar and flour. Add milk and corn syrup; stir to combine. Add margarine. Microwave on HIGH for 3 minutes or until mixture is bubbling. Stir. Microwave on HIGH for 2 minutes longer. To reheat, heat for 30 to 60 seconds or until mixture is warm. Refrigerate any leftover sauce in covered container.

BAD WEATHER DAY

Preparation of these food items is part of the activity of the day. Most of the ingredients are things that would be on hand. "Toad-in-the-Hole" is like a giant popover with sausages in it.

Toad-in-the-Hole

> Toad-in-the-Hole
> Microwave Applesauce
> Frozen Green Beans
> Chocolate Pudding Cake

MEAL PREPARATION SCHEDULE

Early in the day prepare applesauce. About 1 1/4 hours before serving, prepare and bake Chocolate Pudding Cake. About 20 to 25 minutes before it is done, start preparing Toad-in-the-Hole. Bake as soon as oven temperature reaches 425 degrees. About 10 minutes before serving, cook frozen beans, following package directions.

Preparation Time: Toad-in-the-Hole takes 20 minutes to prepare and 25 to 30 minutes to bake. Microwave Applesauce takes 10 to 15 minutes to prepare. Chocolate Pudding Cake takes 15 minutes to prepare and 45 minutes to bake. Green Beans take 10 minutes to cook.

SHOPPING LIST

- 4 to 5 apples
- 1 (12-ounce) package link sausages
- 1 (10-ounce) package frozen green beans
- Ice cream, if desired
- *Check cupboard* for flour, salt, sugar, unsweetened cocoa, baking powder, vegetable oil and brown sugar.
- *Check refrigerator* for butter or margarine, eggs and milk.

Recipes

TOAD-IN-THE-HOLE *(5 servings)*

1 (12-ounce) package link sausages
1/4 cup margarine
3 eggs
1 1/2 cups milk
1 1/2 cups all-purpose flour
3/4 teaspoon salt

Cook sausage in small skillet on stove top according to package directions or place in microwave-safe pie plate; microwave on HIGH for 4 to 5 minutes or until done. Drain on paper towels. (Sausage doesn't have to brown.) Heat oven to 425 degrees. Place margarine in 13x9x2-inch pan; place pan in oven for 2 to 3 minutes to melt margarine. Remove pan from oven. Beat eggs in medium bowl with wire whisk. Stir in milk. Add flour and salt; stir in with spoon until smooth. Arrange cooked sausages in margarine in pan. Pour batter over sausages. Bake for 25 to 30 minutes or until light golden brown.

BAD WEATHER DAY

Toad-in-the-Hole Menu, continued

MICROWAVE APPLESAUCE *(4 to 5 servings)*

4 to 5 apples, peeled and sliced
1/4 cup water
1/4 to 1/2 cup sugar, depending on sweetness of apples

Place apples and water in 2-quart microwave-safe bowl. Cover with waxed paper. Microwave on HIGH until tender, 7 to 8 minutes, stirring once. Stir in sugar. Let stand a few minutes; stir again. Serve warm or cold.

CHOCOLATE PUDDING CAKE *(9 servings)*

While the pudding cake bakes, its own chocolate sauce forms on the bottom of the pan.

1 cup all-purpose flour
3/4 cup granulated sugar
3 tablespoons unsweetened cocoa
2 teaspoons baking powder
1/4 teaspoon salt
1/2 cup milk
2 tablespoons vegetable oil
3/4 cup packed brown sugar
3 tablespoons unsweetened cocoa
1 1/2 cups hot tap water
Ice cream, if desired

Heat oven to 350 degrees. Combine flour, granulated sugar, 3 tablespoons cocoa, baking powder and salt in medium bowl. Add milk and oil; mix well. Pour into ungreased 9x9x2-inch pan. Combine brown sugar and 3 tablespoons cocoa in small bowl; spread evenly over batter in pan. Pour hot water evenly over mixture. Bake for 45 minutes. Cut into 9 pieces while hot; spoon sauce from pan over each serving. Serve with ice cream, if desired.

"The righteous man leads a blameless life; blessed are his children after him."
Proverbs 20:7 (NIV)

BAD WEATHER DAY

Beef Stew

Oven Beef Stew
Teddy Bear Bread
Banana Boats

MEAL PREPARATION SCHEDULE

If bread dough is not thawed, start thawing by 9:00 a.m. Dough will take about 2 hours to thaw, 15 to 20 minutes to shape, 45 minutes to rise and 25 minutes to bake. While dough is rising, after it is shaped and while baking, start cutting up vegetables for stew. Combine ingredients for stew. Stew will take 5 hours to bake, so have in oven by 1:00 p.m. if you want to eat at 6:00 p.m. Don't forget to stir the stew. In late afternoon, make sails for banana boats. Prepare banana boats just before serving.

Preparation Time: Thawed dough takes 15 to 20 minutes to shape; 45 minutes to rise; 25 minutes to bake. Stew takes 20 to 25 minutes to prepare, 5 hours to bake; Banana Boats, 10 minutes to prepare.

(+) indicates that this is the smallest size available; there will be leftovers.

SHOPPING LIST

- 2 pounds cubed beef stew meat
- 1 (14-ounce) can stewed tomatoes
- 1 (10-ounce) package frozen peas
- 1 pound carrots(+)
- 1 bunch celery(+)
- 2 medium onions
- 3 medium potatoes
- 1 (8-ounce) package quick-cooking tapioca(+)
- 1 (8-ounce) can sliced water chestnuts
- 1 package (2 loaves) frozen bread dough(+)
- 1 (15-ounce) package raisins(+)
- 4 bananas
- 1 (8-ounce) can crushed pineapple
- 1 (8-ounce) container frozen whipped topping
- 1 (3-ounce) package chopped nuts
- *Check cupboard* for sugar, salt and pepper.

Recipes

OVEN BEEF STEW *(8 servings)*

2 pounds cubed beef stew meat
1 (14-ounce) can stewed tomatoes
1 (10-ounce) package frozen peas
8 carrots, peeled and sliced
1 cup sliced celery
2 medium onions, chopped
3 medium potatoes, diced
2 tablespoons sugar
2 1/2 teaspoons salt
1/4 teaspoon pepper
1/4 cup quick-cooking tapioca
1 (8-ounce) can sliced water chestnuts, drained

Do not brown meat. Place all ingredients in 5-quart casserole or Dutch oven. Cover with lid or aluminum foil. Bake at 250 degrees for 5 hours. Stir a few times while baking.
(Leftovers can be frozen and served at another meal.)

BAD WEATHER DAY

Beef Stew Menu, continued

TEDDY BEAR BREAD

1 loaf frozen bread dough, thawed*
Raisins

Grease large cookie sheet. Divide dough in half. Shape one half into an oval for bear's body. Place on cookie sheet. Divide remaining dough in half, again. Cut one portion into 6 equal parts and shape into ears, arms and legs. With remaining half of dough, pinch off small amount of dough and roll into a small ball for the nose. Shape remaining dough into a round ball for the head; place at top of body on cookie sheet. Attach nose, arms, legs and ears firmly to body. Add raisins for eyes and buttons, pushing firmly into dough. Cover with plastic wrap. Let rise at room temperature for 45 minutes. Heat oven to 375 degrees. Bake 25 minutes or until light brown and body of bear sounds hollow when lightly tapped.

Thawing method 1: Place frozen bread dough in well-greased bowl. Cover with plastic wrap. Let thaw overnight in refrigerator; in morning leave at room temperature for 30 to 40 minutes before shaping.
Thawing method 2: Heat oven to 200 degrees; turn off. Place frozen bread dough in greased bowl on upper rack in oven. Place bowl of hot water on lower rack. Close oven door. Let dough thaw for about 2 hours. Remove dough from oven; shape.

BANANA BOATS *(4 servings)*

4 bananas
1 (8-ounce) can crushed pineapple, drained
1 (8-ounce) container frozen whipped topping, thawed
1 (3-ounce) package chopped nuts, if desired
Toothpicks and paper

Slice bananas lengthwise. Place 1 banana in each of four serving dishes. Place 1 to 2 tablespoons crushed pineapple on top of each banana. Top pineapple with whipped topping. Sprinkle with nuts. Children can make sails from paper triangles and toothpicks; stick into banana.

"Train a child in the way he should go, and when he is old he will not turn from it."
Proverbs 22:6 (NIV)

The Golden Rule

"Do to others as you would have them do to you."
— Luke 6:31 (NIV)

CHAPTER IV

POTLUCK PARTY DISHES

In my early years of living alone, I always looked forward to potluck parties where I could go and get some decent home cooking. For the small price of taking a box of chips, a six-pack of something, some deli items or a store-bought pie, I could pig-out on a host of homemade casseroles, salads and gooey desserts.

But in simply bringing store-bought stuff, I discovered I was missing the point of it all. In a sense, I felt as if I were cheating... myself, as well as others.

Indeed, I was! A version of the *Golden Rule* is absolutely true in these situations. *"Give to others as you would have them give to you."* In giving one receives. Only I found I received far more than simply good eating.

Working in an office environment I would devote days, weeks and months to an assignment without seeing anything of significance accomplished. Very frustrating and demoralizing. But in two hours at home, I could turn out a deep-dish apple pie that looked as if it could be the home of the nursery rhyme's "four and twenty black-birds!" Humongus! And good! After

sampling a big slab, a national religious leader commented to my friend that I had missed my "calling." No, I didn't, Brother!

While the presence of Divine Love heals the negative feelings one has about oneself, it also helps to receive words of admiration and appreciation from others in the flesh. I found that there is nothing quite so simple, easy and quick to generate such a response as sharing a homemade dish with one's friends.

The comments I've received have ranged from a pleasant "Thank you" to "You made *that* ?" to "Why aren't you married?" I felt sorry for the man who made that last remark. His wife kicked him under the table! Poor guy...she really nailed him!

People, especially women, admire a man who is willing to try and take care of himself. If one is looking for a "cook," I discovered that a very good way to find one, is to be one...first! It seems that cooks attract cooks!

This chapter is loaded with simple recipes that will yield an exciting change in one's life. Try it, you'll like it!

PUNCHES

Five Alive & Squirt *(24 [1/2 cup] servings)*

- 6 (12-ounce) cans Squirt, chilled
- 2 (12-ounce) cans frozen Five Alive concentrate, thawed

In large nonmetal pitcher, combine 3 cans of Squirt with each can of Five Alive. Serve over ice, if desired.

Preparation Time: 5 minutes.

Golden Punch *(25 [1/2-cup] servings)*

- 1 (6-ounce) can frozen pineapple juice concentrate, thawed
- 1 (6-ounce) can frozen lemonade concentrate, thawed
- 1 (12-ounce) can frozen orange juice concentrate, thawed
- 3 cups cold water
- 1 (2-liter) bottle ginger ale, chilled

In large bowl, combine pineapple juice, lemonade concentrate, orange juice and water; stir. Add ginger ale just before serving. Serve over ice, if desired.

Preparation Time: 10 minutes.

Cran-apple Punch *(30 [1/2-cup] servings)*

- 1 (48-ounce) bottle cran-apple juice, chilled
- 1 (6-ounce) can frozen lemonade concentrate, thawed
- 2 cups cold water
- 1 (2-liter) bottle ginger ale, chilled

In large bowl, combine cran-apple juice, lemonade concentrate and water; stir. Add ginger ale just before serving. Serve over ice, if desired.

Preparation Time: 10 minutes.

Tip: Out of ginger ale? Mix equal parts of Coke and 7-Up.

PUNCHES

Hot Creamy Drink *(50 to 60 servings)*

Hot Creamy Drink Mix

- 1 pound butter, softened
- 1 pound (3 1/2 cups) powdered sugar
- 1 pound (2 1/4 cups, packed) brown sugar
- 1 teaspoon cinnamon
- 1/2 gallon vanilla ice cream, softened

In large mixing bowl, combine butter, sugars and cinnamon with electric mixer; blend well. Gradually add ice cream and mix. Freeze until ready to serve.

Preparation Time: 20 minutes.

Hot Creamy Drink Recipe

- 2 tablespoons Hot Creamy Drink Mix
- 1 teaspoon rum flavor extract.
- 1/2 to 2/3 cup boiling water
- Nutmeg, if desired

Place mix in mug or cup. Add rum extract; pour in boiling water to fill mug. Sprinkle with nutmeg. If serving at a party, keep water hot in large electric coffee pot or heat water ahead of time and keep warm in an air pot.

Preparation Time: 5 minutes.

Orange Sherbet Punch *(30 [1/2 cup] servings)*

- 1 quart cold water
- 1 (46-ounce) can pineapple juice
- 1 (6-ounce) can frozen lemonade concentrate, thawed
- 1 (6-ounce) can frozen orange juice concentrate, thawed
- 1/2 gallon orange sherbet
- 1 quart vanilla ice cream
- 1 (2-liter) bottle ginger ale, chilled

Combine water, juice and concentrates in large punch bowl. Add scoops of sherbet and ice cream and ginger ale just before serving.

Preparation Time: 10 minutes.

APPETIZERS

Cereal Snack Mix *(7 cups)*

- 1/4 cup margarine
- 1 tablespoon Worcestershire sauce
- 1/2 teaspoon garlic salt
- 2 cups Wheat Chex cereal* *(1 [16-ounce] package+)***
- 2 cups Rice Chex cereal* *(1 [12-ounce] package+)***
- 2 cups Cheerios* *(1 [10-ounce] package+)***
- 1 cup pretzel sticks *(1 [10-ounce] package+)***
- 1 cup salted mixed nuts or peanuts *(1 [12-ounce] can+)***

Heat oven to 300 degrees. Place margarine in 13x9x2-inch pan. Place pan in oven until margarine is melted. Add Worcestershire sauce and garlic salt; stir to combine. Gradually add cereals, pretzels and nuts, stirring until all pieces are coated. Bake about 45 minutes, stirring every 10 to 15 minutes. Remove from oven and place on several layers of paper towels to cool. Store in tightly covered container.

Preparation Time: 15 minutes to prepare and 45 minutes to bake.

*Any combination of these or other crisp, crunchy unsweetened cereals totaling 6 cups can be used.
** Items in parentheses are minimum amounts to purchase; (+) indicates there will be leftovers.

Deviled Eggs *(24 servings)*

- 12 large eggs
- 1/2 cup mayonnaise or salad dressing
- 1 teaspoon dry mustard
- 1/2 teaspoon salt
- Dash pepper
- Paprika

Hard-cook the eggs a day before or early in the day.

To hard-cook eggs: Place in large saucepan; cover with cold water. Heat to boiling. Reduce heat and simmer 10 minutes. Remove from heat; cover and let stand 10 minutes. Immediately cool eggs in very cold water; let stand 20 to 30 minutes. Allow about 45 minutes after eggs are cooked to prepare filling and fill eggs.

To prepare filling: Peel eggs; cut in half lengthwise. Lift out yolks and place in medium bowl. With a fork, mash yolks. Add mayonnaise, dry mustard, salt and pepper; mix well. With a teaspoon, gently fill egg white halves, slightly rounding tops. Sprinkle with paprika. Cover and refrigerate until serving time.

Cooking/Cooling Time: 1 hour.
Preparation Time: 45 minutes.

Tip: To keep egg yolks from crumbling when slicing hard cooked eggs, wet the knife before each cut.

APPETIZERS

Cheese Dip *(6 to 8 servings)*

- 2 (4-ounce) cans chopped green chilies, drained
- 1 (8-ounce) package (2 cups) shredded Cheddar cheese
- 2 eggs
- 2 tablespoons half-and-half or evaporated milk *(1 [5-ounce] can+)**
- 1 (14-ounce) package tortilla chips

Lightly grease (or spray with no-stick cooking spray) 9-inch pie plate or cake pan. Place chilies in pan. Sprinkle evenly with cheese. In small bowl, beat eggs with fork; stir in milk. Pour egg mixture over cheese. Microwave on MEDIUM-HIGH (70%) power for 10 to 15 minutes or until firm. Cut into small squares and serve on tortilla chips.

Preparation Time: 20 Minutes.

* *Items in parentheses are minimum amounts to purchase; (+) indicates there will be leftovers.*

Spinach Dip *(10 to 12 servings)*

- 1 (10-ounce) package frozen chopped spinach, thawed and squeezed dry in strainer
- 1 envelope dry onion or dry vegetable soup mix
- 1 cup mayonnaise or salad dressing
- 1 (8-ounce) carton dairy sour cream
- 1 (8-ounce) can water chestnuts, drained and chopped
- 1/2 teaspoon Worcestershire sauce

In medium bowl, combine all ingredients. Cover and refrigerate 6 to 8 hours or overnight to blend flavors. Serve with carrot and celery sticks, French bread cubes or ripple potato chips.

Preparation Time: 15 minutes.

APPETIZERS

Cheese Ball *(10 to 12 servings)*

- 1 1/2 cups shredded Chedder cheese *(1 [8-ounce] package+)**
- 1/2 cup crumbled blue cheese *(1 [4-ounce] package+)**
- 1 (8-ounce) package cream cheese, softened
- 2 teaspoons Worcestershire sauce
- 1/4 cup finely chopped onion *(1 small onion)**
- 1 (2-ounce) can mushroom pieces and stems, drained and chopped
- 3/4 cup chopped pecans *(about 3 ounce package)**

In medium bowl, combine cheeses, Worcestershire sauce and onion. With electric mixer at low speed, mix until airy and well blended. Stir in mushrooms. Refrigerate 2 to 3 hours to blend flavors. Place mixture on a piece of plastic wrap, form mixture into a ball; roll in pecans. Wrap in plastic wrap; refrigerate at least 2 hours. Serve with crackers.

Preparation Time: 20 minutes.

Chicken Wings *(48 servings)*

- 24 chicken wings or 48 drumettes or drumies
- 1 cup soy sauce *(1 [10-ounce] bottle+)**
- 3/4 cup packed brown sugar
- 1 (8-ounce) can crushed pineapple, drained
- 1/2 teaspoon garlic salt
- 1/2 teaspoon ground ginger

Heat oven to 350 degrees. If using chicken wings, remove tip of each wing; separate remainder into 2 pieces. Wash chicken in cold water; dry. Place wings in 2 13x9x2-inch pans. Combine remaining ingredients in medium bowl; pour over wings. Bake 30 minutes; turn wings. Bake 30 minutes longer.

Preparation Time: 15 minutes to prepare and 60 minutes to bake.

* Items in parentheses are minimum amounts to purchase; (+) indicates there will be leftovers.

APPETIZERS

Grape Jelly Meatballs *(48 meatballs)*

Meatballs

- 1 pound ground beef
- 1 egg
- 1 small onion, chopped (about 1/4 cup)
- 1/3 cup dry bread crumbs
- 1/4 cup milk
- 3/4 teaspoon salt
- 1/8 teaspoon pepper
- 1 teaspoon Worcestershire sauce

Sauce

- 1 (12-ounce) bottle chili sauce
- 1 (10-ounce) jar grape jelly
- 1 tablespoon lemon juice

Heat oven to 400 degrees. Combine all meatball ingredients in bowl; mix well. Shape into 3/4-inch balls. Place in lightly greased 15 1/2x10x1-inch baking pan. Bake about 15 minutes or until thoroughly baked; drain off fat. Combine sauce ingredients in large saucepan. Heat to boiling over medium heat; reduce heat and simmer 5 minutes. Add meatballs to sauce; stir to coat. Cook over low heat about 30 minutes. Serve warm with toothpicks for spearing.

Preparation Time: 20 minutes to prepare and 45 minutes to bake and heat.

Mexican Meatballs *(40 meatballs)*

- 2 eggs
- 2 pounds ground beef
- 1 (1 1/4-ounce) package taco seasoning mix

In large bowl, beat eggs with fork. Add ground beef and seasoning mix; mix well. Shape into 1-inch balls. Place one-half of meatballs in 15 1/2x10x1-inch baking pan. Bake at 350 degrees for 20 to 25 minutes or until brown; drain off fat. Repeat with remaining meatballs. Serve warm with toothpicks for spearing.

Preparation Time: 25 minutes.
Baking Time: 20 to 25 minutes.

Tip: To shape meatballs, use an ice cream scoop to make uniform balls.

Salads

Quick Potato Salad *(4 to 6 servings)*

- 1 quart water
- 1/2 (32-ounce) package frozen Southern-style hash browns
- 1/2 cup salad dressing or mayonnaise
- 1 teaspoon salt
- 4 green onions, chopped
- 1 teaspoon prepared mustard
- 1 stalk celery, chopped
- 1 teaspoon sugar
- 1/8 teaspoon pepper
- 2 hard-cooked eggs, sliced*

In large saucepan heat water to boiling. Add 1 teaspoons salt, if desired. Add frozen potatoes; cover. Heat to boiling again; reduce heat, cook 2 minutes. Drain well. In large bowl, combine remaining ingredients, except eggs. Mix until smooth. Lightly stir in potatoes to coat with dressing. Cover; refrigerate 3 to 4 hours. Just before serving, garnish with hard-cooked egg slices.

Preparation Time: 20 minutes.
Salad should be made 3 to 4 hours before serving to chill.

**For directions on cooking eggs, see Deviled Eggs recipe, page 48.*

Microwave Fruit Salad *(12 servings)*

- 1 (20-ounce) can pineapple chunks
- 1 tablespoon lemon juice
- 1/3 cup orange juice
- 1 (11-ounce) can mandarin orange segments, drained
- 1 large apple, cut up
- 2 bananas, sliced
- 2 cups seedless green or red grapes *(about 1 pound)**
- 1/2 cup sugar
- 2 tablespoons cornstarch

Drain pineapple; reserve 3/4 cup juice. Place all fruit in large bowl; toss gently to mix. In 2-quart microwave-safe bowl, combine sugar, cornstarch, pineapple juice, lemon juice and orange juice. Microwave on HIGH for 2 to 3 minutes, stirring after each minute until mixture thickens and boils. Boil for 1 minute. Pour hot mixture over fruit. Refrigerate, uncovered, until cool, 1 to 2 hours. Cover and refrigerate several hours or overnight.

Preparation Time: 15 minutes.
Salad should be made several hours ahead to chill.

**Items in parentheses are minimum amounts to purchase; (+) indicates there will be leftovers.*

SALADS

Pasta Salad *(6 to 8 servings)*

- 8 ounces uncooked rainbow pasta wheels *(1 [16-ounce] package+)**
- 8 to 10 cherry tomatoes, halved
- 1 small cucumber, sliced
- 1 small green bell pepper, diced
- 1 medium onion, chopped
- 1/2 teaspoon garlic powder
- 2 teaspoons chopped fresh basil or 3/4 teaspoon dried basil leaves
- 1/2 cup bottled Italian dressing *(1 [8-ounce] bottle+)**
- 1 1/2 tablespoons grated Parmesan cheese

Cook pasta according to package directions; drain and rinse with cold water. Combine all ingredients, except Parmesan cheese, in large bowl. Cover and refrigerate 2 to 3 hours to blend flavors. Just before serving, sprinkle with Parmesan cheese.

Preparation Time: About 25 minutes.
Prepare vegetables while pasta is cooking. Salad should be made 2 to 3 hours before serving to chill.

Layered Lettuce Salad *(10 servings)*

A clear glass baking dish lets you see the layers of the salad

- 1 head lettuce, torn into bite-size pieces
- 1 cup chopped celery
- 1 large green bell pepper, chopped
- 1 medium red onion, sliced
- 1 3/4 cups mayonnaise
- 2 tablespoons sugar
- 3/4 cup shredded Cheddar cheese *(1 [4-ounce] package+)**
- 8 slices bacon, crisply cooked and crumbled** *(8-ounce package+)**

Place lettuce in 13x9x2-inch baking dish or pan. Add layers of celery, green pepper and onion, in that order, over lettuce. Combine mayonnaise and sugar; spread over layers in bowl. Sprinkle cheese, then bacon over mayonnaise. Cover with plastic wrap; refrigerate overnight.

Preparation Time: 20 minutes.
Salad should be made the night before or very early on serving day to allow time to chill.

* Items in parentheses are minimum amounts to purchase; (+) indicates there will be leftovers.
** To cook bacon in a microwave, place paper towel on microwave-safe bacon rack. Place bacon on paper towel; cover with another paper towel. Microwave on HIGH for 8 to 9 minutes or until bacon is done.

CASSEROLES

Layered Turkey Casserole *(10 to 12 servings)*

- 9 uncooked lasagne noodles *(1 [16-ounce] package+)*
- 1 (10 3/4-ounce) can condensed cream of mushroom soup
- 1 (10 3/4-ounce) can condensed cream of chicken soup
- 1 cup dairy sour cream *(1 [8-ounce] carton)*
- 1 cup grated Parmesan cheese
- 1 cup finely chopped onion *(1 large onion)*
- 1 cup sliced ripe olives *(1 [6-ounce] can+)*
- 1 (2-ounce) jar diced pimento, drained
- 1 teaspoon garlic salt
- 4 cups cut-up cooked turkey or chicken *(2-3 pounds, boneless)*
- 4 cups shredded Cheddar cheese *(1 [16-ounce] package)*

Cook lasagne noodles according to package directions. Drain; rinse in hot water. In large bowl, combine soups, sour cream, Parmesan cheese, onion, olives, pimento and garlic salt. Gently stir in turkey or chicken. Grease 13x9x2-inch baking pan or spray with nonstick spray. Place 3 lasagne noodles in bottom of pan. Cover with about one-third of turkey mixture. Sprinkle 1 cup Cheddar cheese evenly over turkey mixture. Repeat layers twice more, ending with cheese layer on top. Bake at 350 degrees for 45 minutes. If made ahead and refrigerated, bake about 60 minutes or until hot and bubbly. Let stand 10 minutes before serving.

Preparation Time: 30 minutes.
Baking/Standing Time: 1 hour and 10 minutes.

Hearty Casserole *(6 to 8 servings)*

- 1 1/2 pounds ground beef
- 1 (10 3/4-ounce) can condensed tomato soup
- 1 soup can of water
- 2 cups unpeeled sliced potatoes *(2 large)*
- 1 cup uncooked regular rice *(1 [16-ounce] package+)*
- 1 medium onion, sliced
- 2 medium stalks celery, sliced
- 1 cup sliced carrots *(2-3 carrots)*

Brown ground beef on top of range in skillet over medium heat, in electric fry pan or in microwave on HIGH for 7 to 8 minutes, stirring 3 times. Drain off fat. In small bowl, combine soup and water. Grease 3-quart casserole or large baking dish. Place ground beef in casserole; top with remaining ingredients, except soup mixture, in order listed. Pour soup mixture over layers. Cover and bake at 350 degrees for about 1 1/2 hours or until hot and bubbly.

Preparation Time: 40 minutes.
Baking/Standing Time: 1 1/2 hours .

* Items in parentheses are minimum amounts to purchase; (+) indicates there will be leftovers.

CASSEROLES

Ham and Cheese Casserole *(10 to 12 servings)*

- 12 slices white bread *(1 loaf+)*
- 2 cups diced ham *(about 1 1/4 pounds)**
- 1 (12-ounce) package (3 cups) shredded Cheddar cheese
- 4 eggs
- 2 cups milk
- 1 tablespoon dry mustard
- 1 teaspoon Worcestershire sauce
- 1 (10 3/4-ounce) can condensed cream of broccoli soup
- 1/2 cup milk

With a knife, trim crusts from bread. Grease 13x9x2-inch baking pan. Arrange 6 bread slices in bottom of pan. Sprinkle with ham and cheese; top with remaining bread slices. In large bowl, beat eggs. Add 2 cups milk, dry mustard and Worcestershire sauce; blend well. Pour mixture over bread slices. Cover with foil; refrigerate 8 to 12 hours or overnight. Bake, covered, at 300 degrees for 1 1/2 hours or until knife inserted near center of pan comes out clean. Let stand 10 minutes before serving. During this time, heat broccoli soup and 1/2 cup milk until hot. Serve broccoli sauce in separate dish for guests to add, if desired.

Preparation Time: 30 minutes; refrigerate overnight 8 to 12 hours.
Baking/Standing Time: 1 hour and 40 minutes.

Quick Tuna Casserole *(6 to 8 servings)*

- 1 (8 or 10-ounce) package egg noodles
- 2 (6 1/2-ounce) cans tuna, drained
- 1 (10 3/4-ounce) can condensed cream of mushroom or celery soup
- 1 cup milk
- 1/2 teaspoon celery seed
- 1 teaspoon onion salt
- 1 (16-ounce) can green peas, drained
- 1 cup shredded Cheddar cheese *(1 [4-ounce] package)**
- Garnish: 3/4 to 1 cup dry bread crumbs, crushed potato chips,
    chow mein noodles, 1 tomato, sliced or 1 green bell pepper, sliced

Heat oven to 375 degrees. Cook egg noodles according to package directions. Meanwhile, combine all other ingredients except garnish. Butter 1 1/2 to 2-quart casserole. Drain noodles; stir into tuna mixture. Pour into casserole. Top with garnish of your choice. Bake 20 to 25 minutes or until casserole is hot and bubbly.

Preparation Time: 15 minutes to assemble; 20 to 25 minutes to bake.

* *Items in parentheses are minimum amounts to purchase; (+) indicates there will be leftovers.*

CASSEROLES

Lasagne *(10 to 12 servings)*

- 1 pound ground beef
- 1 small onion, choped
- 1 green bell pepper, chopped
- 1 (30-ounce) jar spaghetti sauce
- 4 cups shredded mozzarella cheese *(1 [16-ounce] package)* *
- 1 (15-ounce) carton ricotta cheese
- 2 eggs, beaten
- 1/2 teaspoon salt, if desired
- 1/8 teaspoon pepper, if desired
- 1/2 cup water
- 9 uncooked lasagna noodles *(1 [16-ounce] package+)* *

In skillet, brown ground beef, onion and green pepper; drain off fat. Reserve 1 cup of spaghetti sauce. Add remaining spaghetti sauce to ground beef mixture and heat to boiling; reduce heat to low and keep mixture warm. Reserve 1 cup mozzarella cheese. In medium bowl, combine remaining mozzarella cheese, ricotta cheese, eggs, salt and pepper. Combine one third of ground beef mixture with water; spread in bottom of 13x9x2-inch pan. Place 3 lasagna noodles over sauce; top with one third of cheese mixture. Repeat layers 2 more times. Top with reserved sauce and reserved mozzarella cheese. (At this point, lasagna can be covered and refrigerated. Remove cover before baking.) Bake at 350 degrees for about 60 minutes or until thoroughly heated. Let stand 10 minutes before serving.

Variation: Cook lasagna noodles according to package directions; drain and rinse. Omit 1/2 cup water. Follow directions above for layering lasagna. Bake at 350 degrees for about 45 minutes. Let stand 10 minutes before serving.

Preparation Time: 30 minutes.
Baking/Standing Time: 1 hour, 10 minutes.

* *Items in parentheses are minimum amounts to purchase; (+) indicates there will be leftovers.*

"*Example is not the main thing in influencing others. It is the only thing.*"
– Albert Schweitzer

DESSERTS

Mom's Apple Cake *(12 to 15 servings)*

- 4 cups diced, peeled cooking apples *(4 medium apples)**
- 1 cup chopped walnuts *(about 5 ounces)**
- 1 cup raisins *(1 [15-ounce] package+)**
- 2 cups sugar
- 2 eggs
- 1 cup vegetable oil
- 1 teaspoon vanilla
- 2 cups all-purpose flour
- 1 teaspoon baking soda
- 1 teaspoon salt
- 2 teaspoons cinnamon

Heat oven to 350 degrees. Grease 13x9x2-inch cake pan. In large bowl, combine apples, walnuts, raisins and sugar. In separate bowl, beat eggs; stir in oil and vanilla. Add to apple mixture. Combine flour, soda, salt and cinnamon; mix well. Gently stir dry ingredients into apple mixture. Pour into greased pan. Bake 50 to 60 minutes or until wooden toothpick inserted in center comes out clean.

Preparation Time: 30 minutes. Baking Time: 1 hour.

Mississippi Bars *(50 [1 1/2x2-inch] bars)*

Bars

- 1 cup margarine
- 1/2 cup unsweetened cocoa
- 2 cups sugar
- 4 eggs
- 1 1/2 cups all-purpose flour
- Dash salt
- 1 cup chopped nuts *(about 5 ounces)**

Topping and Frosting

- 1 (10-ounce) package miniature marshmallows
- 1/2 cup margarine, softened
- 1/3 cup unsweetened cocoa
- 3 1/2 cups powdered sugar
- 1/3 cup milk
- 1 teaspoon vanilla

Heat oven to 350 degrees. Lightly grease 15 1/2x10x1-inch baking pan. Melt 1 cup margarine in large saucepan over medium heat, or in 2-quart microwave-safe bowl in microwave for 30 to 40 seconds on HIGH. Stir in 1/2 cup cocoa. Stir in sugar, eggs, flour and salt; mix well. Stir in nuts. Spread batter in greased pan. Bake for 18 to 20 minutes. Remove from oven; turn oven off. Arrange marshmallows evenly on top of bars. Return to oven for 5 minutes or until marshmallows are melted. Meanwhile, mix 1/2 cup margarine, 1/3 cup cocoa, powdered sugar, milk and vanilla until well blended and spreading consistency. Frost bars immediately. Cool at room temperature 1 to 2 hours before serving. *(Bars also freeze well.)*

Preparation Time: 25 minutes.
Baking Time: 25 minutes; Cooling Time: 1 to 2 hours.

* Items in parentheses are minimum amounts to purchase; (+) indicates there will be leftovers.

DESSERTS

Caramel - Chocolate Cheesecake *(12 to 14 servings)*

- 2 cups graham cracker crumbs *(1 [13 to 15-ounce] package+)**
- 1/2 cup margarine, melted
- 1 (14-ounce) package caramels
- 1 (5-ounce) can evaporated milk
- 1 cup chopped toasted pecans**
- 2 (8-ounce) packages cream cheese, softened
- 1/2 cup sugar
- 1 1/2 teaspoons vanilla
- 2 eggs
- 1/2 cup semisweet chocolate chips *(1 [6-ounce] package+)**

Heat oven to 350 degrees. In medium bowl, combine crumbs and margarine. Press onto bottom and about 1/2-way up sides of 9-inch springform pan.*** Bake 10 minutes. In 2-quart saucepan, heat caramels and milk over low heat, stirring often until caramels are melted. Pour melted caramel mixture over crust. Sprinkle with pecans. In large bowl, combine cream cheese, sugar and vanilla; beat with electric mixer until well blended. Add eggs, one at a time, beating well after each addition. Stir in chocolate chips. Pour mixture over pecans. Bake about 40 minutes or until set. Cool 10 minutes. Remove sides of pan. Cool completely. Cover and refrigerate.

Preparation Time: 30 to 35 minutes.
Baking Time: 40 to 50 minutes; at least 4 hours to chill.

* Items in parentheses are minimum amounts to purchase; (+) indicates there will be leftovers.
**To toast pecans, place on pie plate; toast for about 15 minutes at 300 degrees, stirring occasionally.
***A 9x9x2-inch pan can be substituted for a springform pan. Line with 2 strips of foil placed at right angles to each other so foil overhangs on all sides for ease in removing cheesecake from pan.

Nutty Fudge *(64 [1-inch] pieces)*

- 1 (12-ounce) package peanut-butter-flavored chips
- 1 cup milk chocolate chips *(1 [11 1/2-ounce] package+)**
- 1/4 cup butter or margarine
- 1 (14-ounce) can sweetened condensed milk *(not evaporated)*
- 1/2 cup chopped salted peanuts *(about 4 ounces)*

Lightly butter 8x8x2-inch pan. Place peanut butter chips, chocolate chips, butter and sweetened condensed milk in 2-quart microwave-safe bowl. Microwave at MEDIUM (50% power) for 3 to 4 minutes or until chips have melted. (*Chips melted in a microwave keep their shape, so be sure to stir the chips to see if they have melted.*) Stir in peanuts. Pour into buttered pan. Refrigerate until set. Cut into squares.

Preparation Time: 10 minutes.
Refrigerate 30 to 45 minutes to chill.

* Items in parentheses are minimum amounts to purchase; (+) indicates there will be leftovers.

DESSERTS

Apple Pie *(8 servings)*

- Pastry for 9-inch 2-crust pie*
- 1/2 cup packed brown sugar
- 1/4 cup granulated sugar
- 2 tablespoons flour
- 1/2 teaspoon cinnamon
- 1/4 teaspoon ground nutmeg
- 6 cups sliced, peeled tart baking apples *(6 apples)***
- 1 tablespoon lemon juice

Heat oven to 425 degrees. Prepare pie crust; keep well covered. In large bowl, combine sugars, flour, cinnamon and nutmeg. Add apples and lemon juice; toss until well combined. Place apples in pastry-lined pie pan. Cover with top crust. Fold and roll top edge under bottom edge; press together to seal edge; flute if desired. Cut slits in top of crust to allow steam to escape. Bake for 40 to 45 minutes. Cool on wire rack for at least 60 minutes.

Preparation Time: 50 to 60 minutes for crust and pie filling.
Bake 45 minutes. Cool 60 minutes.

Raisin-Pecan Pie *(8 servings)*

- Pastry for 9-inch, one-crust pie*
- 3 eggs
- 2/3 cup sugar
- 1/2 teaspoon salt
- 1/2 teaspoon ground cinnamon
- 1/2 teaspoon ground nutmeg
- 1/2 teaspoon ground cloves
- 1 cup dark corn syrup *(1 [16-ounce] bottle+)***
- 1/3 cup butter, melted
- 1/2 cup chopped pecans *(about 2 ounces)***
- 1/2 cup raisins *(1 [15-ounce] package+)***

Heat oven to 375 degrees. Prepare pastry. Beat eggs, sugar, salt, cinnamon, nutmeg, cloves, corn syrup and butter with hand beater until blended. Stir in pecans and raisins. Pour into pastry-lined pie plate. Bake until set, 40-50 minutes.

Preparation Time: 30 minutes for crust and pie filling.
Bake 50 minutes. Cool 60 minutes.

*Packaged pie crust mix, refrigerated pie crusts or the Successful Pie Crust recipe, page 60, can be used.
** Items in parentheses are minimum amounts to purchase; (+) indicates there will be leftovers.

DESSERTS

SUCCESSFUL PIE CRUST *(2 one-crust pies or 1 two-crust pie)*

- 2 cups all-purpose flour
- 1/4 teaspoon salt
- 2/3 cup shortening
- 1 egg, beaten
- 2 tablespoons water
- 2 teaspoons lemon juice

In medium bowl, combine flour and salt. With pastry blender or two knives, cut in shortening until pieces are the size of small peas. In small bowl, beat egg, water and lemon juice until well mixed. Gradually add to flour mixture, until all flour is moistened and dough cleans side of bowl. With your hands, form dough into a ball. Divide dough into 2 parts. *(If making one-crust pie, remaining dough can be frozen.)*

To roll pastry, flatten 1 ball of dough on lightly floured, cloth-covered surface. With floured rolling pin, roll dough from center to edges, until 2 inches larger than inverted pie plate. Wrap pastry around rolling pin; unroll into pie plate. Ease pastry into pie plate; do not stretch pastry. *(The floured cloth keeps the pastry from sticking to the board without adding more flour to the pastry.)*

One-crust pie: Using kitchen scissors, trim overhanging edge of pastry 1 inch from rim of pie plate. Fold and roll pastry under, even with pie plate; make a fluted edge. Fill and bake as directed in recipe. For baked shell, prick bottom and side thoroughly with fork. Bake at 475 degrees for 8 to 10 minutes.

Two-crust pie: Turn desired filling into pastry-lined pie plate (as above). Trim overhanging edge of pastry 1/2 inch from rim of pie plate. Roll second part of dough. Wrap pastry around rolling pin; unroll over filling. Cut slits so steam can escape. Trim overhanging edge of pastry 1 inch from rim of pie plate. Fold and roll top edge under lower edge, pressing on rim to seal securely; flute if desired. Bake as directed in recipe.

Preparation Time: About 10 minutes.

"Success is going from failure to failure with no loss of enthusiasm."
– Winston Churchill

POTLUCK PARTY TABLE SETUP

The arrangement of the table for a potluck party is mostly a matter of convenience. If the meal is to be served on a table against a wall, the arrangement illustrated below (A) is common. Begin at one end of the table with plates, then move on in order to meat or main dish, vegetables, salad, bread, condiments, silverware and finally napkins. Guests should finish at end of table nearest sitting-eating area.

If the table is in the center of the room, it can be arranged to have two lines with duplicate service on both sides of the table, or it can be arranged as illustrated below (B) where guests walk around entire table.

One-Sided Table Service (A)

Full Table Service (B)

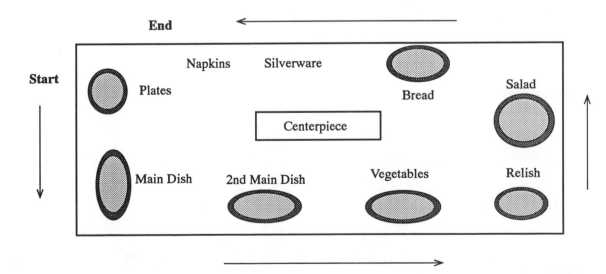

"Men want to be a woman's first love; women have a more subtle instinct: they want to be a man's last romance." — Unknown

CHAPTER V

JUST FOR TWO

The title of the introduction to this cookbook, *"From Burnt Offerings to Melted Hearts,"* comes from an episode when I tried to prepare a romantic dinner for two. I really wanted to impress her by being a super cool dude in the kitchen.

I wasn't and it didn't! Dinner preparation, including the food, was a complete and utter catastrophe! Nothing turned out right. Even the squirrels on my deck wouldn't touch it!

For some unknown reason, I selected a complicated fish kabob dinner complete with hush puppies. It was one of those menus where everything is to be started and finished at the last minute at the same time. That was the first mistake!

All the recipes were new to me, and I got behind immediately. In hurrying, I managed to mess up the hush puppy recipe. When I tried to "fix" it, I only made matters worse. I got further behind. Meanwhile the fish kabobs were starting to burn! Too late! They went up in smoke! In the end, I abandoned the hush puppies. The kabobs amounted to flacky loose slivers of fish that fell off the skewers, and the vegetable chunks became little charcoal briquettes.

I was nearly in tears from frustration and exasperation over the way this affair was turning out. She *was* in tears, watching me struggle trying to keep it together for her sake!

From this experience I learned that the old adage, *"the way to a man's heart is through his stomach,"* is equally true for a woman. However, it's not the food *per se* that matters to her.

Well, it does, but it doesn't. Taking time from your schedule in planning the menu, shopping, and preparing the meal tells her she is special. It makes her feel cherished. It will likely melt her heart!

If the meal turns out right, rejoice! If it doesn't, don't worry about it. You have already given her a powerful message that you care about her.

There is nothing quite so intimate and romantic as a meal just for two. It can also be a real adventure! The menus in this chapter should serve you well.

ROMANTIC DINNER FOR TWO

Beef Tips

Beef Tips with Noodles
Whole Green Beans
Waldorf Salad
Crusty Rolls
Mini Fruit Pizza
Flavored Coffee

MEAL PREPARATION SCHEDULE

About 3 hours before serving, prepare Beef Tips. Set table. About 1 hour before serving, prepare Waldorf Salad and Fruit Pizza. About 15 minutes before serving, cook noodles and prepare beans according to package directions.

Preparation Time: Beef Tips, 10 minutes to prepare; 2 1/2 to 3 hours to bake. Waldorf Salad, 15 minutes to prepare. Fruit Pizza, 15 minutes to prepare. Beans and noodles, 10 to 15 minutes to cook.

SHOPPING LIST

- 3/4 pound cubed beef stew meat
- 1 (10 3/4-ounce) can condensed cream of mushroom soup(+)
- 1 (16-ounce) bottle red cooking wine
- 1 (2.5-ounce) package dry onion soup mix(+)

SHOPPING LIST, *continued*

- 1 (2.5-ounce) jar sliced mushrooms
- 1 (8-ounce) package egg noodles(+)
- 1 (10-ounce) package frozen whole green beans
- 2 to 4 crusty rolls
- 1 large red apple
- 1 bunch celery(+)
- 1 (2 1/2-ounce) package chopped nuts(+)
- 1 (3-ounce) package cream cheese
- 2 large bakery sugar cookies
- Fresh fruit for pizza (see recipe)
- 1/4 pound coffee (*e.g. French Vanilla*)
- *Check cupboard* for powdered sugar and almond extract.
- *Check refrigerator* for lettuce, lemon juice, mayonnaise or salad dressing.
- Flower centerpiece (Flowers of the season, arranged low to the table)

(+) *indicates that this is the smallest size available; there will be leftovers.*

Recipes

BEEF TIPS WITH NOODLES *(2 servings)*

3/4 pound cubed beef stew meat
1/2 (10 3/4-ounce) can condensed cream of mushroom soup
1 (2.5-ounce) jar sliced mushrooms, drained
1/2 cup red cooking wine
1/2 envelope dry onion soup
4 ounces egg noodles

Do not brown meat. Place all ingredients, except noodles, in greased 1-quart casserole; mix well. Cover and bake at 325 degrees for 2 1/2 to 3 hours, stirring occasionally. About 15 minutes before serving, cook noodles according to package directions; drain. Serve beef mixture over noodles.

ROMANTIC DINNER FOR TWO

Beef Tips Menu, continued

WALDORF SALAD *(2 servings)*

2 lettuce leaves
1 large unpeeled red apple
1 small stalk celery, chopped
1/4 cup chopped nuts
1 teaspoon lemon juice
1/4 cup mayonnaise or salad dressing

Wash and drain lettuce leaves; refrigerate to crisp. Core and chop apple. In medium bowl, combine all ingredients except lettuce; stir gently. Cover and refrigerate until serving time. Just before serving, spoon half of salad onto each lettuce leaf.

MINI FRUIT PIZZAS *(2 servings)*

1 (3-ounce) package cream cheese, softened
2 tablespoons powdered sugar
1/8 teaspoon almond extract
2 or 3 of the following fruits:
   Sliced strawberries
   Fresh blueberries
   Fresh raspberries
   Sliced kiwi fruit
   Halved red or green seedless grapes
   Sliced bananas
2 large bakery sugar cookies

Combine cream cheese, powdered sugar and almond extract until smooth. Wash fruit and drain well on paper towels. Carefully spread cream cheese mixture on cookies. Arrange fruit over cream cheese. Place on a plate, cover loosely with plastic wrap; refrigerate until serving time.

"A wife of noble character who can find? She is worth far more than rubies.
Her husband has full confidence in her and lacks nothing of value.
She brings him good, not harm, all the days of her life."
Proverbs 31:10-12 (NIV)

ROMANTIC DINNER FOR TWO

Baked Fish

Baked Fish with Broiled Topping
Baked Potato
Broccoli Salad
Apple Crisp
Flavored Coffee

MEAL PREPARATION SCHEDULE

If using frozen fish, remove from freezer and place in refrigerator to thaw the night before serving. Bacon can be cooked the night before and refrigerated. *If using microwave,* prepare food in this order: potato, apple crisp, fish, salad. *If using oven,* begin baking potato 1 hour before serving; quickly prepare apple crisp and place in oven; 20 minutes before serving, place fish in oven, finish making salad, beat egg white and add tartar sauce. Remove potato, apple crisp and fish from oven. Spread egg-white mixture over fish and broil.

Preparation Time: Oven; 1 hour, 15 minutes. Microwave; 30 minutes.

SHOPPING LIST

- 2 (4 to 5-ounce) orange roughy, cod or other white fish fillets
- 1 (8-ounce) jar tartar sauce(+)
- 1 (8-ounce) package bacon(+)

SHOPPING LIST, *continued*

- Fresh broccoli (from salad bar or 1 small bunch)
- 1 small red onion
- 1 (15-ounce) package raisins(+)
- Sunflower seeds (from salad bar) or 1 (4-ounce) package(+)
- 2 large cooking apples
- 2 medium to large white baking potatoes (russet)
- 1 (18-ounce) carton quick-cooking rolled oats(+)
- 1/4 pound coffee *(e.g. Butter Pecan or Cinnamon)*
- *Check cupboard* for salt, pepper, vinegar, granulated sugar, brown sugar, flour and cinnamon.
- *Check refrigerator* for butter or margarine, lemon juice, eggs, mayonnaise and salad dressing.
- Flower centerpiece (Flowers of the season, arranged low to the table)

(+) *indicates that this is the smallest size available; there will be leftovers.*

Recipes

BAKED OR MICROWAVED FISH *(2 servings)*

2 (4- to 5-ounce) orange roughy, cod or other white fish fillets
2 tablespoons margarine or butter
Dash salt and pepper
2 to 4 tablespoons tartar sauce
1 egg white for oven fish

ROMANTIC DINNER FOR TWO

Baked Fish Menu, continued

Thaw fish in refrigerator overnight or in microwave for 3 to 4 minutes on DEFROST. (Be careful not to cook fish.) If portion is still frozen, run under cold water for a few minutes until thawed. Melt butter in microwave on HIGH for 30 seconds or in baking pan in oven. Salt and pepper fish and coat with melted butter.

Oven Method: Bake at 350 degrees for 15 to 20 minutes or until fish flakes with a fork. While fish is baking, in small mixing bowl with wire whisk or electric mixer, beat egg white, salt and pepper until stiff peaks form. With a spoon, gently fold in tartar sauce. Remove fish from oven. Spread egg white mixture on fish and broil about 4 inches from heat source for 2 minutes or until golden brown. Serve with tartar sauce, if desired.

Microwave Method: Place fish in microwave-safe dish with thickest part of fish to the outside. Pour on melted butter. Cover with waxed paper. Microwave on HIGH for 4 to 5 minutes or until fish flakes with a fork. Serve with tartar sauce, if desired.

BAKED POTATOES *(2 servings)*

2 medium to large white baking potatoes (russet)

Scrub potatoes with vegetable brush. Prick with fork for steam to escape. *Oven Method:* Bake until potato is easily pierced with fork, about 1 1/2 hours at 350 degrees. *Microwave Method:* Place paper towel in microwave; place potato on towel, not in center of oven. Microwave on HIGH for 6 to 8 minutes. Remove from microwave and wrap in foil or a towel to keep heat in and to finish cooking. *(Skin of microwaved potato will not be as crisp as oven-baked potato.)*

BROCCOLI SALAD *(2 servings)*

4 slices bacon
2 cups broccoli pieces
1 small red onion, sliced
4 teaspoons raisins
2 tablespoons sunflower seeds
3 tablespoons mayonnaise or salad dressing
2 teaspoons sugar
1/2 teaspoon vinegar or lemon juice

Place bacon between 2 paper towels on microwave-safe rack or dish. Microwave on HIGH for 2 to 5 minutes or fry in skillet; drain. Cool, crumble and set aside. In medium bowl, combine broccoli, red onion, raisins and sunflower seeds. In separate bowl, combine mayonnaise, sugar and vinegar. Toss broccoli with dressing mixture. Sprinkle with bacon. Refrigerate if not serving immediately.

(continued, next page)

ROMANTIC DINNER FOR TWO

Baked Fish Menu, continued

APPLE CRISP *(2 servings)*

2 large cooking apples
1/2 teaspoon lemon juice
2 tablespoons margarine or butter
2 tablespoons brown sugar
2 tablespoons quick-cooking rolled oats
3 tablespoons flour
1/2 teaspoon cinnamon

Oven Method: Heat oven to 350 degrees. Peel, core and slice apples into 9-inch pie plate. Sprinkle with lemon juice. In small bowl, combine remaining ingredients; stir with fork until crumbly. Sprinkle over apples, bake for 35 minutes or until apples are tender.
Microwave Method: Peel, core and slice apples into 2-cup microwave-safe bowl. Sprinkle with lemon juice. Combine remaining ingredients until crumbly. Sprinkle over apples. Microwave on HIGH for 4 to 5 minutes or until apples are tender.

'In Him all things hold together.'
Col. 1:17

ROMANTIC DINNER FOR TWO

Chicken Tortellini Soup

Chicken Tortellini Soup
Easy Biscuits
Chocolate Truffles
Flavored Coffee

MEAL PREPARATION SCHEDULE

About 30 minutes before serving, begin to prepare soup. Meanwhile, prepare biscuits according to package directions for drop or rolled-out biscuits. Make coffee. Place truffles on small plate or dish.

Preparation Time: Soup, 15 minutes; Biscuits, 10 minutes. Cooking/Baking Time: Soup, 15 minutes; Biscuits, 10 minutes.

(+) indicates that this is the smallest size available; there will be leftovers.

SHOPPING LIST

- 1 small onion
- 1 (14 1/2-ounce) can chicken broth
- 1 (9-ounce) package refrigerated or frozen cheese tortellini(+)
- 1 (10-ounce) package frozen peas(+)
- 8 ounces cooked, diced chicken (from deli)
- 1/4 pound coffee *(e.g. Hazelnut Truffle)*
- 1 (24-ounce) bottle 100% white grape juice.
- Chocolate truffle candies
- *Check cupboard* for vegetable oil and baking mix.
- *Check refrigerator* for garlic and milk.
- Flower centerpiece (Flowers of the season, arranged low to the table)

Recipes

CHICKEN TORTELLINI SOUP *(2 servings)*

1 tablespoon vegetable oil
1 small onion, chopped
2 teaspoons minced garlic
1 (14 1/2-ounce) can chicken broth
1/2 cup 100% white grape juice
1 cup (about 4 ounces) refrigerated or frozen cheese tortellini
1/3 cup frozen peas
1 cup diced, cooked chicken

In large saucepan, heat oil over medium heat. Add onion and garlic; cook and stir until onion is soft. Add chicken broth and grape juice; cover and heat to boil.. Uncover; stir in tortellini and peas. Return to boiling; add chicken. Reduce heat and simmer 8 to 10 minutes.

EASY BISCUITS *(2 servings)*

Prepare rolled or drop biscuits from baking mix, following package directions.

WEEKEND BREAKFAST

Cheese Omelet

Cheese Omelet
Muffins with Honey Butter
Fresh Strawberries
Almost Orange Julius

MEAL PREPARATION SCHEDULE

Prepare Honey Butter the day before. About 25 minutes before serving, remove Honey Butter from refrigerator and wash strawberries in cold water; let drain. Place all Almost Orange Julius ingredients, except ice cubes, in blender; do not blend. Make coffee. Wrap muffins in paper towel; place in microwave. Prepare omelet. Heat muffins 10 to 15 seconds on HIGH. Add ice cubes to blender and blend. Serve strawberrries with powdered sugar.

Preparation Time: Omelet, 5 to 10 minutes; Strawberries, 5 minutes; Orange Julius, 5 minutes; Honey Butter, 10 minutes.

SHOPPING LIST

- 1 (4-ounce) package shredded Cheddar cheese(+)
- 1 (6-ounce) can frozen orange juice concentrate
- 2 to 4 bakery muffins
- 1 pint fresh strawberries
- *Check cupboard* for salt, pepper, honey, sugar, vanilla, cinnamon, nutmeg and powdered sugar.
- *Check refrigerator* for eggs, butter or margarine and milk.
- *Check freezer* for ice cubes.

(+) *indicates that this is the smallest size available; there will be leftovers.*

Recipes

CHEESE OMELET *(2 servings)*

4 eggs
4 teaspoons water
1/4 teaspoon salt
Dash pepper
4 teaspoons butter
2 ounces (1/2 cup) shredded Cheddar cheese

In small bowl, beat eggs, water, salt and pepper with fork for about 20 seconds; eggs should not foam. Melt butter in medium skillet over medium-high heat, tilting skillet to coat surface. Add egg mixture; reduce heat to low. As omelet sets, lift edge to allow any uncooked egg mixture on top to flow under the cooked omelet. (An omelet should be light brown on the outside and set, but not liquid on the inside.) Sprinkle cheese on center of omelet. Gently loosen omelet edge and fold in half over cheese. Place on serving plate.

Tip: For a fluffier omelet, add a dash of cornstarch before beating eggs.

WEEKEND BREAKFAST

Cheese Omelet Menu, continued

ALMOST ORANGE JULIUS *(4 servings)*

1 (6-ounce) can frozen orange juice concentrate, thawed
1 cup milk
1 cup water
4 to 6 tablespoons sugar
1/2 teaspoon vanilla
10 to 12 ice cubes

Combine all ingredients in blender. Cover and blend until smooth.

HONEY BUTTER, *(3/4 cup)*

1/2 cup butter, softened
1/4 cup honey
1/2 teaspoon cinnamon
Dash nutmeg

In small bowl, beat butter with electric mixer. Slowly add honey, cinnamon and nutmeg. Continue beating until well mixed and creamy. Cover and refrigerate until serving time.

"Charm is deceptive, and beauty is fleeting;
but a woman who fears the Lord is to be praised.
Give her the reward she has earned,
and let her works bring her praise at the city gate."
Proverbs 31:30, 31 (NIV)

PICNIC

Turkey-Wild Rice Salad

Turkey-Wild Rice Salad
Fruit Kabobs
Croissant
Cupcakes
Iced Flavored Coffee

MEAL PREPARATION SCHEDULE

Cook wild rice the day before so it can be chilled. Prepare salad dressing at least 2 hours before serving. Prepare kabobs and refrigerate. Combine rice and salad ingredients, except dressing. Make coffee, cool over ice and pour into thermos. Pack salad, dressing and kabobs in insulated cooler with an ice pack. Before serving, toss salad with dressing.

Preparation Time: Rice takes about 10 minutes to prepare; about 45 minutes to cook. Salad takes about 25 minutes to assemble. Kabobs take about 15 minutes to prepare.

(+) indicates that this is the smallest size available; there will be leftovers.

SHOPPING LIST

- 1 pint(+) or 8 medium-sized strawberries
- 1 small bunch green seedless grapes
- 1 (8-ounce) can pineapple chunks
- 1 (11-ounce) can mandarin orange segments
- Bamboo skewers
- 1 (14 1/2-ounce) can chicken broth *(not condensed)*
- 1 (16-ounce) package wild rice(+)
- 1/2 pound smoked turkey breast
- 1 bunch green onions(+)
- 1 pint cherry tomatoes(+)
- 1 (3-ounce) package sliced almonds(+)
- 1 (12-ounce) bottle tarragon wine vinegar(+)
- Bakery croissants
- Bakery cupcakes
- 1/4 pound coffee *(e.g. Cinnamon Hazelnut)*
- *Check cupboard* for sugar, dried tarragon leaves, garlic salt, dry mustard and vegetable oil.
- *Check refrigerator* for lettuce.

Recipes

FRUIT KABOBS *(4 kabobs)*

8 medium-sized strawberries
16 to 20 green seedless grapes
1 (8-ounce) can pineapple chunks, drained
1 (11-ounce) can mandarin orange segments, drained
4 bamboo skewers

Wash strawberries and grapes; drain well. Alternate fruit pieces on skewers. Keep cool.

PICNIC

Turkey-Wild Rice Salad, continued

TURKEY-WILD RICE SALAD *(2 servings)*

Salad

1 (14 1/2-ounce) can chicken broth
1/2 cup uncooked wild rice, rinsed and drained
1/2 pound smoked turkey breast, cubed
2 green onions, chopped
4 to 5 cherry tomatoes, halved
2 tablespoons sliced almonds
2 crisp lettuce leaves, washed

Dressing

1 teaspoon dried tarragon leaves
1/2 teaspoon garlic salt
1/2 teaspoon sugar
1/4 teaspoon dry mustard
3 tablespoons vegetable oil
2 tablespoons tarragon wine vinegar

Heat chicken broth to boiling in medium-sized heavy saucepan. Stir in rice; cover. Reduce heat; simmer about 40 minutes or until rice is tender. Uncover; fluff with a fork. Simmer 5 minutes; drain. Cover and refrigerate until thoroughly chilled. *(There will be about 1 1/2 cups of cooked rice.)*

Combine all dressing ingredients in tightly covered jar; shake well. Refrigerate 2 to 3 hours to blend flavors.

Mix wild rice, turkey, onions, tomatoes and almonds in large bowl. Just before serving, add dressing to salad mixture; stir to blend well. Serve on lettuce leaves.

Remember the tablecloth, plates, napkins, flatware and glasses!

"Where has your lover gone, most beautiful of women?
Which way did your lover turn, that we may look for him with you?
My lover has gone down to his garden, to the beds of spices,
to browse in the gardens and to gather lilies.
I am my lover's and my lover is mine;
he browses among the lilies."
Song of Songs 6:1-3 (NIV)

"Honor your father and mother...that it may go well with you and that you may enjoy long life on the earth." — Ephesians 6: 2,3 (NIV)

CHAPTER VI

VERY SPECIAL OCCASIONS

"For better or for worse, for richer or for poorer, in sickness and in health, ..." mothers, valentines and secretaries are a substantial and important part of our lives. They are very special people. Secretaries are essential; valentines are by choice, and mothers are with us from birth, *"...'til death do us part."*

A whole page (page 80) is devoted to secretaries.

My Valentine is a secret....

And my mom died several years ago. She was a good friend...I miss her.

It wasn't always that way. Indeed, I'm sure that if, as a rebellious and arrogant young man, I had asked her permission to be born, she would have likely said, "No!" It took the better part of thirty-five years to convince her otherwise.

The turning point in our relationship came when I sought her forgiveness for the selfish things I had said and done that had hurt her. Her response was immediate! "Oh, Bob, I forgive you for every little thing!"

The sweetest words I've ever heard! And the most important. Everything was different from that moment on. The slate was wiped clean.

To be sure, we had our disagreements about this and that. But the previous resentment and mistrust were replaced by a new respect and understanding for each other. And, surprisingly, I discovered someone I'd never known before–a funny lady, a real character. I learned that when she'd bark at me the best response was to bark right back! She loved it!

In tribute to her, her Ham Loaf recipe is included in this chapter and her Apple Cake recipe is on page 57. Both are excellent! Enjoy!

MOTHER'S DAY

Mom's Ham Loaf

Mom's Ham Loaf
Baked Potatoes
Peas and Carrots
Lemon-Lime Gelatin Salad
Strawberry Shortcake
Flavored Coffee

MEAL PREPARATION SCHEDULE

Prepare salad the night before so it will set. If making shortcake, bake ahead and warm up shortly before serving. On the day of the dinner, prepare ham loaf and baked potatoes and place in oven. Prepare sauce for ham loaf. While meal is baking, set table, clean lettuce and strawberries. Whip cream, if necessary, and refrigerate. Cook peas and carrots. Cut salad into serving pieces and place on lettuce leaves on individual salad plates. Just before serving dessert, spoon strawberries onto shortcakes.

Preparation Time: Ham Loaf, 20 minutes to prepare and 1 1/2 hours to bake. Salad, 15 minutes to prepare, refrigerate overnight. Potatoes, 10 minutes to prepare and 1 1/2 hours to bake. Vegetables 15 minutes to cook. Strawberry Shortcake, 15 minutes to prepare.

SHOPPING LIST

- 8 medium to large white baking potatoes (russet)
- 1 pound ground ham
- 1 1/2 pounds lean ground pork
- 1 (16-ounce) package frozen peas and carrots
- 1 (3-ounce) package lemon-flavored gelatin
- 1 (3-ounce) package lime-flavored gelatin
- 1 (16-ounce) can pear halves
- 1 quart fresh strawberries
- 1/2 pint whipping cream, 1 (4-ounce) carton frozen whipped topping or half & half
- Bakery angel food cake, yellow sponge cake cups or home-baked biscuit shortcake from baking mix
- 1/2 pound coffee *(e.g. French Vanilla)*
- *Check cupboard* for bread crumbs, vinegar, brown sugar, dry mustard and sugar.
- *Check refrigerator* for butter or margarine, eggs, milk and lettuce.

Recipes

BAKED POTATOES *(8 servings)*

8 medium to large white baking potatoes (russet)

Scrub potatoes with vegetable brush. Prick with fork for steam to escape. Bake until potatoes are easily pierced with fork, about 1 1/2 hours at 350 degrees.

MOTHER'S DAY

Mom's Ham Loaf Menu, continued

MOM'S HAM LOAF *(8 servings)*

1 pound ground ham
1 1/2 pounds lean ground pork
1 cup dry bread crumbs
1 egg, beaten
1 cup milk
1/2 cup vinegar
1/2 cup water
3/4 cup packed brown sugar
1 teaspoon dry mustard

In large bowl, combine ham and pork. In separate bowl, combine crumbs, egg and milk; let stand to allow crumbs to soak up moisture. Gently mix crumb mixture into ground meat; shape into loaf. Place in roasting pan without a rack. Bake at 350 degrees for 30 minutes. Meanwhile, in saucepan, combine vinegar, water, brown sugar and dry mustard. Heat to boiling over low heat. Boil, stirring occasionally, until sauce is thickened. Spoon about 1/4 sauce over ham loaf; bake about 1 hour longer, spooning on 1/4 of sauce every 15 minutes.

LEMON-LIME GELATIN SALAD *(8 servings)*

1 (3-ounce) package lemon-flavored gelatin
1 (3-ounce) package lime-flavored gelatin
2 cups boiling water
1 (16-ounce) can pear halves
Lettuce leaves

Combine lemon- and lime-flavored gelatins in 9-inch square pan. Add boiling water; stir until gelatin is dissolved. Drain pears, reserving liquid. Add water to pear liquid to measure 1 3/4 cups. Stir liquid into gelatin mixture. Refrigerate until slightly thickened. Arrange pear halves, cut side down, in gelatin. Refrigerate until firm. Cut into squares; serve on lettuce.

STRAWBERRY SHORTCAKE *(8 servings)*

1 quart fresh strawberries
1/4 to 1/2 cup sugar (depending on sweetness of berries)
1/2 pint whipping cream, 1 (4-ounce) container frozen whipped
   topping, thawed, or half & half
Shortcake: use slices of bakery angel food cake, purchased
   yellow sponge cake cups or prepare shortcakes from baking
   mix, following package directions

Wash strawberries in cold water, drain; remove stems. Slice berries into a bowl; sprinkle with sugar and stir gently. At serving time, spoon strawberries onto shortcake. Whip cream with 1 tablespoon sugar, if desired; spoon onto shortcakes or serve shortcakes with half & half.

VALENTINE'S DAY

Creamy Chicken

> Creamy Chicken
> Twice-Baked Potatoes
> Peas with Pearl Onions
> Lettuce Wedge with Choice of Dressing
> Bread or Muffins
> Cherry Cheese Tarts
> Flavored Coffee

MEAL PREPARATION SCHEDULE

The night before or early in the day, prepare Cherry Cheese Tarts. (Or make ahead and freeze.) About 2 1/2 hours before serving, begin preparing Creamy Chicken and bake. Then scrub potatoes and place in oven. Prepare Lettuce Wedges and chill. Set table. Thirty minutes before serving, finish potato preparation. Cook Peas and Pearl Onions according to package directions. At dessert time, serve Cherry Cheese Tarts with flavored coffee.

Preparation Time: Creamy Chicken takes 15 minutes to prepare and 2 1/4 hours to bake. Potatoes take 15 minutes to prepare and 1 3/4 hours to bake. Lettuce Wedges take 10 minutes to prepare. Peas and Pearl Onions take about 5 minutes to prepare and 10 minutes to cook. Cherry Cheese Tarts take 15 minutes to prepare and 15 minutes to bake; they must be chilled before serving.

(+) indicates that this is the smallest size available; there will be leftovers.

SHOPPING LIST

- 4 skinless, boneless chicken breast halves
- 1 (8-ounce) package bacon(+)
- 1 (4-ounce) package dried beef(+)
- 1 (10 3/4-ounce) can condensed cream of mushroom soup(+)
- 1 (8-ounce) carton dairy sour cream(+)
- 2 large baking potatoes (russet)
- 1 (4-ounce) package shredded Cheddar cheese(+)
- 1 (16-ounce) package peas and pearl onions
- 1 small head lettuce
- 1 (8-ounce) bottle salad dressing of your choice(+)
- Bread or muffins from bakery
- 1 (12-ounce) package vanilla wafers(+)
- 1 package foil baking cups (muffin/cupcake pan liners)
- 1 (8-ounce) package cream cheese
- 1 (21-ounce) can cherry pie filling
- 1/2 pound coffee *(e.g. Black Forest Chocolate or Caffe Amaretto)*
- *Check cupboard* for salt, pepper, paprika, sugar and vanilla.
- *Check refrigerator* for milk, butter or margarine and eggs.

Recipes

CREAMY CHICKEN *(4 servings)*

4 skinless, boneless chicken breast halves
4 slices bacon
1/2 (4-ounce) package dried beef
1/2 (10 3/4-ounce) can condensed cream of mushroom soup
1/2 cup dairy sour cream

VALENTINE'S DAY

Creamy Chicken Menu, continued

Wash chicken; pat dry with paper towels. Wrap each chicken breast half with a slice of bacon. Arrange dried beef slices in 9x9x2-inch baking dish or casserole. Place chicken over slices, making sure bacon ends are secured under chicken pieces. In small bowl, combine soup and sour cream; spoon over chicken. Bake uncovered at 325 degrees for 2 1/4 hours. Casserole can be assembled, covered and refrigerated several hours before baking; remove cover before baking.

TWICE-BAKED POTATOES *(4 servings)*

2 large white baking potatoes (russet)
1/4 cup milk
2 tablespoons butter or margarine
1/2 teaspoon salt
1/4 teaspoon pepper
1/4 cup shredded Cheddar cheese
Paprika

Scrub potatoes and prick with fork. Place in oven and bake at 325 degrees until potatoes are easily pierced with a fork, about 1 3/4 hours. Remove potatoes from oven and cut in half lengthwise. Scoop out inside of potato, leaving a thin shell. Place scooped out potato in bowl; mash with electric mixer until no lumps remain. Beat in milk in small amounts. Add butter, salt and pepper; beat until smooth and fluffy. Spoon mixture back into potato skins; mixture will mound up in skins. Sprinkle with cheese and paprika. Place potatoes in pie plate or shallow baking dish. Return to 325 degree oven until cheese melts.

LETTUCE WEDGES *(4 servings)*

1 small head iceberg lettuce
Bottled salad dressing

Remove and discard outer leaves from lettuce. Remove core. Wash lettuce; drain. Cut lettuce into 4 wedges. Just before serving, place wedges on individual salad plates. Serve with dressing.

CHERRY CHEESE TARTS *(12 tarts)*

12 vanilla wafers
12 foil baking cups (muffin/cupcake pan liners)
1 (8-ounce) package cream cheese, softened
1/4 cup sugar
1 egg
1 teaspoon vanilla
1 (21-ounce) can cherry pie filling

Heat oven to 350 degrees. Place 1 vanilla wafer in the bottom of each foil baking cup; place baking cups on cookie sheet. With electric mixer, beat cream cheese, sugar, egg and vanilla 5 minutes; mixture should be smooth and creamy. Spoon mixture into baking cups, filling each about half full. Bake 12 to 15 minutes. Cool. Spoon cherry pie filling over mixture in each cup. Refrigerate until serving time. (*Leftover tarts can be frozen.*)

SECRETARIES' WEEK IDEAS

I quickly learned that cooking is much like golf or tennis. It's an acquired skill that requires practice. Since I lived alone, I took advantage of the situation and turned my office into a test kitchen. My co-workers would eat anything, and have a good time doing it!

Well, almost anything. The worst test was a huckleberry pie. A co-worker and I took one bite, looked at each other and shook our heads, "No!" I took the "thing" to the men's room and flushed it!

Other than that, my cooking was a treat for the office personnel and did wonders for my self-esteem and self-confidence. What started out as a bi-monthly little treat grew into coordinating office pie-baking and Christmas cookie contests in conjunction with the annual community fund-raising drives.

It was amazing to see how seriously people considered these contests and the amount of work they went to in preparing for them. One woman was reduced to tears when her fancy Christmas cookies didn't win! During a pie-baking contest, one of the male judges publicly declared he wanted to elope with the maker of pie #6. Not a smooth move. Pie #6 was mine!

Another unexpected reward surfaced. Cooking for my co-workers raised the *esprit de corps* of the office from virtually nothing to a little bit of something ... at least for a few moments. While supplying homemade treats to the office doesn't exactly fit a business school MBA image, it does win hearts. Big time!

So, the place to start is in your own little cubicle with a plate of Nutty Fudge (page 58), and a sign that says, "Help yourself!" At first, people won't believe you. Their response will be, "What do you want?" Don't be discouraged, just keep at it.

Next, share Mom's Apple Cake (page 57) with your division or section. Then, on to the word processing center and/or the computer center. These two groups are often the unsung heroes of an organization. A little goody on a regular basis will guarantee you a spot at or near the front of the line. It's not bribery, it's gratefulness. Make every week Secretaries' Week!

In addition to the potluck dishes (Chapter IV), feel free to select recipes from other menus and serve them as separate dishes. Below are a few suggestions to get you started. Remember to expand them to the number of people you are serving.

Salads

Waldorf Salad	*65*
Broccoli Salad	*67*
Molded Cranberry Salad	*84*

Hot Dishes

Pizza Casserole	*32*
Cheese-Ham Quiche	*86*
Broccoli-Corn Bake	*127*

Desserts

Peanut Butter-Chocolate Chip Cookies	*26*
Saint Croix River Bottom Dessert	*115*
Frosted Lemon Bars	*129*

CHAPTER VII

HOLIDAY MEALS WITH FAMILY OR FRIENDS

Cook-and-do-dishes! Cook-and-do-dishes! Cook-and-do-dishes!

For three days straight, it's cook-and-do-dishes!

"Are we having a good time, yet?"

Yes, and no. Holidays are a bittersweet time for me. Sweet in terms of spending time with family and friends. But bitter in terms of being reminded of the consequences of a broken family.

I have this mystical picture in my mind of a Norman Rockwell kind of traditional family setting. Mom and Dad are seated at the banquet table surrounded by happy, squeaky-clean faces, young and old, smiling with love and adoration for one another, in eager anticipation of devouring the feast set before them.

Don't I wish!

I remember the first few Thanksgivings, Christmases and Easters separated from my family after my divorce. I was so lonesome I thought I was going to die and wished I could. While I was often with other well-meaning family members and/or friends, they could not compensate for my heartache.

To be sure there are families that do fit the traditional picture. I envy them. But in today's world of broken families and many remarriages, holidays can be trying times at best.

However mystical it may seem, I continue to believe in the traditional family structure. There is a simplicity, goodness and rightness about it that cannot be denied.

As with each family, there is a special and unique spirit about my family. While we don't fit the traditional structure, we are fortunate and blessed to have an all-for-one, one-for-all unity. I see it as my responsibility to maintain that unity of spirit in the bond of peace.

The message of Christmas and Easter is real to me. I've learned that God is in the business of reconciling families. While it couldn't be done in total, He saved a remnant for me! I'm pleased He did.

In keeping with tradition, the menus in this chapter are the conventional ones. Some might bust the budget. Who cares? It's Christmas!

THANKSGIVING DINNER

Roast Turkey Breast

> Roast Turkey Breast with Stuffing
> Mashed Potatoes and Gravy
> Squash with Lemon-Pepper Butter
> Molded Cranberry Salad
> Dinner Rolls
> Pumpkin Pie with Whipped Cream
> Flavored Coffee

MEAL PREPARATION SCHEDULE

Two days before Thanksgiving, place turkey in refrigerator to thaw. The day before, prepare pie and salad. Wash lettuce leaves; wrap in paper towels and put in plastic bag to crisp. About 1 1/4 hours before serving, begin preparing squash; peel and cook potatoes if using fresh. Prepare stuffing as directed on package for 8 servings; place in casserole and bake or microwave. Arrange lettuce on salad plates; cut salad and place on lettuce. During 10 minute turkey-standing time, mash potatoes or prepare instant potatoes and make gravy.

Preparation Time: Thaw turkey 2 days before; takes about 10 minutes to prepare and 3 to 3 3/4 hours to bake; Potatoes, 20 minutes to prepare and 25 minutes to cook; Squash, 15 minutes to prepare and 60 minutes to bake; Pumpkin Pie, 25 minutes to prepare and 55 minutes to bake; Salad, about 15 minutes to prepare, and several hours to set.

SHOPPING LIST

- 5 to 6-pound frozen turkey breast
- 1 bunch green onions(+)
- 10 medium potatoes or 1 (20-serving) package instant mashed potatoes(+)
- 1 (4-pound) buttercup squash
- 1 (7-ounce) package dry stuffing mix

SHOPPING LIST, *continued*

- 1 bunch celery for stuffing, if desired
- 1 (20-ounce) can crushed pineapple
- 1 (3-ounce) package lemon-flavored gelatin
- 1 (3-ounce) package raspberry-flavored gelatin
- 2 (7.5-ounce) bottles frozen lemon juice(+) or 3 to 4 lemons
- 2 (16-ounce cans) whole berry cranberry sauce
- 1 (2 1/2-ounce) package walnut pieces
- 1 (8-ounce) carton dairy sour cream(+)
- Dinner rolls from bakery
- 1 package refrigerated all-ready pie crusts or frozen deep dish pie crusts in pans
- 1 (16-ounce) can pumpkin (*not pumpkin pie filling*)
- 1 (12-ounce) can evaporated milk (*not sweetened condensed*)
- 1/2 pint whipping cream or 1 (4-ounce) container frozen whipped topping
- 1/2 pound coffee (*e.g. Butter Pecan or any toasted flavor*)
- *Check cupboard* for salt, pepper, vegetable oil, flour, brown sugar, granulated sugar, cinnamon, cloves, nutmeg and ginger.
- *Check refrigerator* for milk, butter or margarine, mayonnaise, lettuce and eggs.
- Table centerpiece (Thanksgiving theme)

(+) *indicates that this is the smallest size available; there will be leftovers.*

THANKSGIVING DINNER

Roast Turkey Breast Menu, continued

Recipes

ROAST TURKEY BREAST *(8 servings)*

5- to 6-pound frozen turkey breast, thawed
2 to 3 tablespoons vegetable oil
1 to 2 tablespoons lemon juice
Salt and pepper
4 green onions, trimmed

Rinse turkey breast in cold water; pat dry. Brush all sides with oil, then lemon juice. Lightly salt and pepper turkey breast. Insert green onions in breast cavity. Place turkey breast on rack in shallow baking pan. Bake at 325 degrees for 1 to 1 1/4 hours or until lightly browned. Cover with a tent of aluminum foil; continue baking 2 to 2 1/2 hours longer or until meat thermometer reaches 180 degrees. Remove turkey from oven and let stand, covered with foil, for about 10 minutes for ease in slicing.

MASHED POTATOES *(8 servings)**

10 medium potatoes
1 teaspoon salt
1/4 cup butter or margarine
1 cup milk

Peel potatoes, removing any "eyes"; rinse in cold water. Quarter potatoes. Place in saucepan and cover with water. Heat to boiling; cover, reduce heat and simmer over low heat for about 25 minutes or until tender. Drain well. Using potato masher or electric mixer, mash potatoes. After they are broken up, add salt, butter and 1/2 cup milk. Whip with mixer, gradually adding additional milk as necessary, until fluffy.
* *If using instant mashed potatoes, follow package directions for 8 servings.*

SQUASH WITH LEMON-PEPPER BUTTER *(8 servings)*

1 (4-pound) buttercup squash
1/2 cup butter
2 tablespoons lemon juice
2 teaspoons pepper
1 teaspoon salt
1/4 cup packed brown sugar

Cut squash in half; remove seeds. Cut each half into 2 pieces. Place on cookie sheet skin side down. Dot each piece with 1 tablespoon butter. Bake at 325 degrees for 1 hour. Scoop squash out of skin; place in large bowl and mash. Stir in remaining butter, lemon juice, pepper and salt. Sprinkle with brown sugar.

(continued, next page)

THANKSGIVING DINNER

Roast Turkey Breast Menu, continued

GRAVY *(2 1/4 cups)*

1/4 cup turkey drippings (fat and juices)
1/4 cup flour
2 cups liquid (turkey juices, broth or water)
Salt and pepper to taste

Place turkey breast on warm platter; keep warm while preparing gravy. Pour drippings from pan into bowl, leaving brown particles in pan. Return 2 tablespoons drippings to pan. (Measure carefully because not enough fat makes lumpy gravy.) Stir in flour. (It is important to have equal amounts of drippings and flour to keep gravy from being greasy.) Cook over low heat, stirring constantly until mixture is smooth and bubbly; remove from heat. Stir in liquid. Heat to boiling, stirring constantly. Boil and stir 1 minute. Season with salt and pepper.
(If gravy is too thick, thin with additional liquid. If too thin, thicken with additional flour dissolved in cold water; heat to boiling, boil and stir 1 minute.)

MOLDED CRANBERRY SALAD *(9 to 12 servings)*

1 (20-ounce) can crushed pineapple
1 (3-ounce) package lemon-flavored gelatin
1 (3-ounce) package raspberry-flavored gelatin
1/2 cup lemon juice
2 (16-ounce) cans whole berry cranberry sauce
1/3 cup chopped walnuts
1/2 cup mayonnaise
1/2 cup dairy sour cream
Lettuce leaves, washed

Drain pineapple, reserving liquid. Add water to liquid to measure 1 1/2 cups. Heat liquid to boiling. Combine lemon and raspberry gelatin in 9x9x2-inch square pan. Add boiling liquid; stir until gelatin is dissolved. Stir in pineapple, lemon juice, cranberry sauce and walnuts. Refrigerate until set. For dressing, combine mayonnaise and sour cream. Place lettuce leaves on individual salad plates. Cut salad into squares; place on lettuce. Serve with dressing.

THANKSGIVING DINNER

Roast Turkey Breast Menu, continued

PUMPKIN PIE *(9-inch pie)*

Pastry for 9-inch one-crust pie *(see Successful Pie Crust recipe, page 60)*,
   or 1 package refrigerated all-ready pie crusts.*
1 (16-ounce) can pumpkin *(not pumpkin pie filling)*
2 eggs, beaten
1 (12-ounce) can evaporated milk *(not sweetened condensed)*
1/2 teaspoon salt
3/4 cup sugar
1 teaspoon cinnamon
1/4 teaspoon nutmeg
1/8 teaspoon ground cloves
1/8 teaspoon ginger
1/2 pint whipping cream or 1 (4-ounce) container frozen whipped
   topping, thawed, if desired

Heat oven to 425 degrees. Line pie plate with pastry. (Refrigerate or freeze remaining pie crust for another use.) In bowl, combine remaining ingredients except whipping cream; beat until smooth. Pour into pie shell. Bake at 425 degrees for 10 minutes; reduce oven temperature to 350 degrees and bake 40 to 45 minutes or until knife inserted near center comes out clean. If desired, cover edge of pie with strip of aluminum foil to prevent excessive browning; remove last 15 minutes of baking time. Cool on wire rack. Whip cream, adding 1 tablespoon sugar, if desired. Top servings of pie with whipped cream, or pass so guests can serve themselves.
* *Frozen deep dish pie crust in foil pan can be substituted for pastry.*

Psalm 100
A Psalm for Giving Thanks

Shout for joy to the Lord, all the earth.
Serve the Lord with gladness; come before him
with joyful songs.
Know that the Lord is God. It is he who made
us, and we are his; we are his people, the sheep
of his pasture.
Enter his gates with thanksgiving and his courts
with praise; give thanks to him and praise his
name.
For the Lord is good and his love endures
forever; his faithfulness continues through all
generations.

CHRISTMAS BREAKFAST

Cheese-Ham Quiche

Cranberry Raspberry Juice
Cheese-Ham Quiche
Christmas Tree Rolls
Hot Cocoa with Candy Cane Stirrers
Flavored Coffee

MEAL PREPARATION SCHEDULE

The day before, prepare rolls and refrigerate for baking on Christmas morning or bake and reheat on Christmas morning. Prepare cocoa mix, chill or reconstitute juice and chill. On Christmas morning, bake rolls, prepare quiche. Remove rolls from oven; cool. Meanwhile, reduce oven temperature and bake quiche. Spread icing on rolls and heat water for cocoa.

Preparation Time: Quiche takes about 10 minutes to prepare and 50 minutes to bake. Rolls take about 30 minutes to prepare (the day before) and 25 to 30 minutes to bake or 10 minutes to warm.

(+) indicates that this is the smallest size available; there will be leftovers.

SHOPPING LIST

- 1 (48-ounce) bottle cran-raspberry juice cocktail or 1 (12-ounce) can frozen cranberry-raspberry juice concentrate
- 1 package refrigerated all-ready pie crusts or frozen deep dish pie crusts in pans
- 1 (6-ounce) package sliced cooked ham
- 1 (4-ounce) package shredded Cheddar cheese
- 1 (12-ounce) can evaporated milk *(not sweetened condensed)*
- 1 strip (3 packages) active dry yeast(+)
- Candy canes
- Red and green candied cherries
- 1/2 lb. flavored coffee *(e.g. Irish Creme)*
- *Check cupboard* for dry mustard, flour, salt, pepper, sugar, cinnamon, powdered sugar and vanilla.
- *Check refrigerator* for eggs, butter or margarine and milk.

Recipes

CHEESE-HAM QUICHE *(6 servings)*

1 package refrigerated all-ready pie crusts or frozen deep dish
  pie crusts in pans *(or use Successful Pie Crust recipe, page 60)*
1 (6-ounce) package cooked ham, chopped
4 ounces (1 cup) shredded Cheddar cheese
4 eggs
1 cup undiluted evaporated milk
1 1/2 teaspoons dry mustard
1/4 teaspoon salt
1/8 teaspoon pepper

Heat oven to 350 degrees. Line 9-inch pie pan with pastry. (Refrigerate or freeze remaining crust for another use.) Sprinkle ham and cheese in pie shell. In bowl, beat eggs; stir in milk, dry mustard, salt and pepper. Pour over ham and cheese. Bake 45 to 50 minutes or until center is set. If edge of pie crust browns too quickly, cover with a narrow strip of foil.

CHRISTMAS BREAKFAST

Cheese-Ham Quiche Menu, continued

CHRISTMAS TREE ROLLS *(1 Christmas Tree)*

Rolls

3 to 3 1/4 cups all-purpose flour
1 package active dry yeast
1/4 cup sugar
3/4 teaspoon salt
2 tablespoons butter or margarine,
   softened
1/2 cup milk
1/3 cup water
1 egg, beaten

Filling

1/2 cup sugar
1 teaspoon cinnamon
2 tablespoons margarine or butter, melted

Icing and Decoration

1 cup powdered sugar
1 to 2 tablespoons milk
1 1/2 teaspoons butter or margarine,
   softened
1/8 teaspoon vanilla
Red and green candied cherries

In large bowl, combine 1 1/2 cups flour, yeast, 1/4 cup sugar and salt; stir to blend. Add 2 tablespoons margarine. Heat milk and water to 120 to 130 degrees (very warm to the touch). Add liquid to flour mixture. With electric mixer on medium speed, beat 2 minutes, scraping bowl. Add egg and 1 cup flour. Beat at high speed 1 minute. With wooden spoon, gradually stir in remaining flour until dough leaves side of bowl. On floured surface, knead for about 5 minutes or until dough is smooth and elastic. Cover with plastic wrap and let rest 20 minutes.

Meanwhile, cover cookie sheet with foil; grease foil. In small bowl, combine 1/2 cup sugar and 1 teaspoon cinnamon. Punch down dough. On lightly floured surface, with rolling pin, roll dough into 8x16-inch rectangle. Spread with 2 tablespoons melted butter and sprinkle with sugar-cinnamon mixture. Beginning with wide side of dough, roll up. Pinch edges to seal. Cut into sixteen 1-inch pieces. Arrange slices with sides of slices touching and cut sides down, on foil-lined cookie sheet, in tree shape (1 in the first row, 2 in second row, 3 in third row, 4 in fourth row, 5 in fifth row and 1 for trunk). Cover with plastic wrap and refrigerate from 2 to 24 hours.

About 20 minutes before baking, heat oven to 375 degrees. Remove rolls from refrigerator, remove plastic wrap and let stand at room temperature 20 minutes. Bake 25 to 30 minutes or until golden brown. Remove rolls from cookie sheet; let cool. Combine all icing ingredients in bowl; mix until smooth and spreading consistency. Frost tree and decorate with candied cherries.

(Tip: Rolls can also be baked in greased 13x9x2-inch baking pan. Recipe can be easily doubled to make 2 trees or 1 pan of rolls and 1 tree.)

COCOA

See page 25 for Cocoa Mix Recipe

Stir with candy canes for a festive touch and peppermint flavor.

CHRISTMAS DINNER
(High Budget Menu)

Standing Beef Rib Roast

Shrimp Cocktail
Standing Beef Rib Roast
Parsley Buttered or Browned Potatoes
Green Bean Casserole
Fresh Fruit Salad
Dinner Rolls
Peppermint Ice Cream Pie
Flavored Coffee

MEAL PREPARATION SCHEDULE

The day before, prepare Peppermint Ice Cream Pie and freeze. About 2 1/2 hours before serving, start Standing Rib Roast. Prepare shrimp and refrigerate. Prepare potatoes. Prepare oranges, kiwi and pomegranate for salad; refrigerate. About 50 minutes before serving start preparing green beans. Remove roast from oven when done and let stand 10 to 15 minutes before carving. Melt butter if making Parsley Buttered Potatoes. Slice apples and combine with other fruit for salad. Remove pie from freezer 10 minutes before cutting.

Preparation Time: Shrimp Cocktail takes about 10 minutes to prepare plus time to chill. Roast takes about 10 minutes to prepare and 2 to 2 1/2 hours to roast. Potatoes take 10 to 20 minutes to prepare and 20 to 45 minutes to cook. Green Bean Casserole takes 10 minutes to prepare and 40 minutes to bake. Fresh Fruit Salad takes 15 to 20 minutes to prepare. Ice Cream Pie takes 15 to 20 minutes to make and 5 hours to freeze.

SHOPPING LIST

- 3 to 4 dozen frozen medium shrimp
- 1 (12-ounce) bottle cocktail sauce
- 1 (4- to 6-pound) standing beef rib roast

SHOPPING LIST, *continued*

- 1 1/2 to 2 pounds new potatoes
- 1 bunch fresh parsley(+)
- 2 (16-ounce) cans French-style green beans
- 1 (10 3/4-ounce) can condensed cream of mushroom soup
- 1 (2.8-ounce) can fried onion rings
- 2 large crisp red apples
- 2 large green or yellow apples *(Granny Smith or Golden Delicious)*
- 3 to 4 oranges
- 2 kiwi fruit
- 1 star fruit
- 1 pomegranate
- Dinner rolls from bakery
- 1/2 gallon pink peppermint ice cream
- 1 prepared chocolate or graham cracker pie crust
- 1 can or jar of your favorite chocolate or hot fudge sauce
- Whipping cream or frozen whipped topping, if desired
- 1/2 pound coffee *(e.g. Butter Rum)*
- *Check refrigerator* for butter or margarine.
- Table centerpiece (Christmas theme)

(+) *indicates that this is the smallest size available; there will be leftovers.*

CHRISTMAS DINNER

Standing Beef Rib Roast Menu, continued

Recipes

SHRIMP COCKTAIL *(6 to 8 servings)*

3 to 4 dozen medium cooked or uncooked frozen shrimp
1 (12-ounce) bottle cocktail sauce

If shrimp is cooked, thaw under cold running water following package directions. If shrimp is uncooked, cook according to package directions, usually 2 1/2 to 3 minutes. Chill before serving. Serve with cocktail sauce, in small bowls or lettuce cups.

STANDING BEEF RIB ROAST *(6 to 8 servings)*

4- to 6-pound standing beef rib roast

Place roast in roasting pan, using ribs to form the rack. Insert meat thermometer; avoid touching the bone or fat pocket. Roast at 325 degrees, uncovered for 2 to 2 1/2 hours. Meat thermometer should read 140 degrees for rare and 160 degrees for medium. Let roast stand 10 minutes before carving. Remove any fat from meat juice and drippings. Add about 1/2 cup water to juices in pan; heat and stir over medium heat until juice is hot, using a spoon to scrape the bottom of the pan. Serve with meat.

PARSLEY BUTTERED POTATOES *(6 to 8 servings)*

1 1/2 to 2 pounds new potatoes
1/3 cup butter, melted
1/3 cup chopped fresh parsley

Wash potatoes and peel thin strip around center of each potato. Place potatoes in saucepan and cover with water. Heat to boiling. Cook until tender, 15 to 20 minutes. Drain. Place in serving bowl and pour butter over potatoes. Sprinkle with parsley.

BROWNED POTATOES *(6 to 8 servings)*

1 1/2 to 2 pounds new potatoes

Peel potatoes. Place in pan with roast about 45 minutes before roast is done. Baste with juices from roast. Bake until tender, 45 to 60 minutes, basting about 3 times. (Small potatoes will dry out quickly.)

(continued next page)

CHRISTMAS DINNER

Standing Beef Rib Roast Menu, continued

GREEN BEAN CASSEROLE *(6 to 8 servings)*

2 (16-ounce) cans French-style green beans
1 (10 3/4-ounce) can condensed cream of mushroom soup
1 (2.8-ounce) can fried onion rings, crushed

Drain beans; place in 2-quart casserole. Add soup and about half of the onion rings. Sprinkle remaining onion rings on top. Bake at 325 degrees for 35 to 40 minutes or until heated thoroughly.

FRESH FRUIT SALAD *(8 servings)*

3 to 4 oranges
2 large crisp red apples, washed
2 large green or yellow apples, washed
    (Granny Smith or Golden Delicious)
2 kiwi fruit, peeled and sliced
1 star fruit, washed and sliced
1/2 cup pomegranate seeds

Peel oranges; cut into slices, then cut each slice into 4 pieces; place in large bowl. Remove apple cores; slice apples into bowl. Add kiwi and star fruit to apples. Toss gently. Peel off pomegranate skin; remove and save the seeds, discarding white membrane. Sprinkle promegranate seeds on top.

PEPPERMINT ICE CREAM PIE *(8 servings)*

1/2 gallon pink peppermint ice cream
1 prepared chocolate or graham cracker pie crust
1 can or jar chocolate or hot fudge sauce
Whipped cream or frozen whipped topping, thawed, if desired

The day before, or at least 5 hours ahead of serving, soften ice cream slightly. Gently spoon into pie shell. Cover with plastic wrap and freeze. Remove from freezer about 10 minutes before serving to aid in cutting. Cut into 8 wedges; place each on an individual dessert plate. Serve with chocolate sauce and whipped cream.

Christmas

In those days Caesar Augustus issued a decree that a census should be taken of the entire Roman world. (This was the first census that took place while Quirinius was governor of Syria.) And everyone went to his own town to register.

So Joseph also went up from the town of Nazareth in Galilee to Judea, to Bethlehem the town of David, because he belonged to the house and line of David. He went there to register with Mary, who was pledged to be married to him and was expecting a child. While they were there, the time came for the baby to be born, and she gave birth to her firstborn, a son. She wrapped him in strips of cloth and placed him in a manger, because there was no room for them in the inn.

And there were shepherds living out in the fields nearby, keeping watch over their flocks at night. An angel of the Lord appeared to them, and the glory of the Lord shone around them, and they were terrified. But the angel said to them, "Do not be afraid. I bring you good news of great joy that will be for all the people. Today in the town of David a Savior has been born to you; he is Christ the Lord. This will be a sign to you: You will find a baby wrapped in strips of cloth and lying in a manger."

Suddenly a great company of the heavenly host appeared with the angel, praising God and saying,

"Glory to God in the highest, and
on earth peace to men on whom his
favor rests."

When the angels had left them and gone into heaven, the shepherds said to one another, "Let's go to Bethlehem and see this thing that has happened, which the Lord has told us about."

So they hurried off and found Mary and Joseph, and the baby, who was lying in the manger. When they had seen him, they spread the word concerning what had been told them about this child, and all who heard it were amazed at what the shepherds said to them. But Mary treasured up all these things and pondered them in her heart. The shepherds returned, glorifying and praising God for all the things they had heard and seen, which were just as they had been told.

On the eighth day, when it was time to circumcise him, he was named Jesus, the name the angel had given him before he had been conceived.

Luke 2:1-21 (NIV)

CHRISTMAS DINNER
(Lower Budget Menu)

Beef Pot Roast

Beef Pot Roast with Potatoes and Carrots
Brown and Serve Rolls
Strawberry Salad
Red and Green Sundaes
Christmas Cookies
Flavored Coffee

MEAL PREPARATION SCHEDULE

Cookies can be made a day or two ahead, or earlier, and frozen. The day before, make the salad and refrigerate (it sets up quickly). About 3 hours before serving time, brown meat. While meat is cooking, clean and cut potatoes and carrots. Add vegetables to meat and cook according to recipe 1 1/4 to 1 1/2 hours before serving. Arrange cookies on serving plate. Remove meat from oven; bake rolls as directed on package. After meal, dish up ice cream and add topping.

Preparation Time: Roast takes about 15 minutes to prepare and 2 1/2 hours to bake. Salad takes about 10 minutes to prepare. Cookies take 50 minutes to prepare and bake. Rolls take about 6 minutes to bake.

SHOPPING LIST

- 4- to 5-pound beef blade or chuck roast
- 1 medium onion
- 7 to 8 medium potatoes
- 1 pound carrots

SHOPPING LIST, *continued*

- 1 (12-ounce) package brown and serve rolls
- 1 (3-ounce) package strawberry-flavored gelatin
- 1 (10-ounce) package frozen strawberries
- 1 (4-ounce) container frozen whipped topping
- 1 (10 1/2-ounce) package miniature marshmallows(+)
- 1 (3-ounce) package cream cheese
- Red- and green-colored sugars(+)
- 1 quart vanilla ice cream
- 1 small bottle grenadine syrup or green creme de menthe
- 1/2 pound coffee *(e.g. Chocolate Mint)*
- *Check cupboard* for salt, pepper, shortening, granulated and powdered sugar, vanilla, flour, cream of tartar and baking soda.
- *Check refrigerator* for eggs, butter or margarine.
- Table centerpiece (Christmas theme)

(+) *indicates that this is the smallest size available; there will be leftovers.*

Recipes

BEEF POT ROAST WITH POTATOES AND CARROTS *(6 to 8 servings)*

4- to 5-pound beef blade or chuck roast
1 teaspoon salt
1/2 teaspoon pepper
1 medium onion, sliced
1 cup water
7 to 8 medium potatoes, peeled, halved
7 to 8 medium carrots, peeled, quartered

CHRISTMAS DINNER

Beef Pot Roast Menu, continued

In Dutch oven or roaster over medium heat, brown both sides of pot roast. Sprinkle with salt and pepper. Add onion and water. Cover and bake at 325 degrees for 1 hour. Add potatoes and carrots; cover and bake 1 1/4 to 1 1/2 hours longer, or until meat and vegetables are tender.

STRAWBERRY SALAD WITH TOPPING *(6 servings)*

1 (3-ounce) package strawberry-flavored gelatin
1 cup boiling water
1 (10-ounce) package frozen strawberries, partially thawed
1 (4-ounce) container frozen whipped topping, thawed
3/4 cup miniature marshmallows
1 (3-ounce) package cream cheese, softened* .

Dissolve gelatin in boiling water. Stir in strawberries and juice. Pour into serving bowl; refrigerate until firm. Gently blend whipped topping, marshmallows and cream cheese together. Spread over gelatin; refrigerate until serving time.
* *To soften cream cheese in microwave, remove from wrapper, place on microwave-safe plate and microwave on DEFROST for 30 to 40 seconds.*

RED AND GREEN ICE CREAM SUNDAES

Scoop ice cream into individual dishes. Pour a little grenadine or creme de menthe over each serving or pass in pitchers so guests can serve themselves.

EASY CHRISTMAS SUGAR COOKIES *(5 to 6 dozen)*

1 cup butter or margarine
1 cup shortening
1 cup granulated sugar
1 cup powdered sugar
2 eggs, slightly beaten
1 teaspoon vanilla
4 1/2 cups all-purpose flour
1 teaspoon salt
1 1/4 teaspoons cream of tartar
1 1/4 teaspoons baking soda
Red- and green-colored sugars

Heat oven to 350 degrees. With electric mixer in large bowl, combine butter and shortening. Gradually add granulated and powdered sugars, mixing until well blended. Add eggs and vanilla; mix well. Stir in flour, salt, cream of tartar and baking soda. Using teaspoon, form into balls. Place red and green sugars in separate small bowls. Dip balls into either colored sugar; place on ungreased cookie sheets. Flatten slightly with hand. Bake 10 to 12 minutes or until set and light brown on edges.

New Year's Eve

Beef Fondue Menu

Beef Fondue with Sauces
Parmesan Cheese Bread
Spinach Salad
Chocolate Cake
Flavored Coffee

MEAL PREPARATION SCHEDULE

Two days before, heat chicken broth mixture and chill. The day before or early in the day make cake, cook bacon, wash spinach and refrigerate. Frost cake when cool. About 1 1/2 hours before serving, cube beef, cut tomatoes and green onions for salad, make dressing for salad and refrigerate. Set table. Place sauces in serving bowls. Twenty minutes before serving, prepare bread. Heat broth and toss salad. When broth is heated, pour into fondue pot and light fondue burner. Serve cake on individual plates.

Preparation Time: Fondue takes about 20 minutes to prepare, salad about 25 minutes to prepare, bread about 20 minutes to prepare, cake 20 minutes to prepare, 35 minutes to bake, 15 minutes to make frosting and frost cake.

(+) indicates that this is the smallest size available; there will be leftovers.

SHOPPING LIST

- 1 (14 1/2-ounce) can chicken broth *(not condensed)*
- 1 (24-ounce) bottle 100% white grape juice
- 1 medium and 1 small onion
- 1 bunch celery(+)
- 1 bunch fresh parsley(+)
- 2 pounds beef sirloin
- 1 loaf French bread
- 1 (10-ounce) package fresh spinach
- 3 medium tomatoes
- 1 bunch green onions
- 1 (8-ounce) can sliced water chestnuts
- 1 (8-ounce) package bacon(+)
- Fuel for fondue pot
- Fondue sauces (see recipe)
- 1/2 pound coffee *(e.g. Jamaican Certified)*
- *Check cupboard* for salt, pepper, garlic, dried tarragon, bay leaf, Worcestershire sauce, paprika, Parmesan cheese, cider vinegar, granulated sugar, powdered sugar, vegetable oil, flour, baking powder, baking soda, unsweetened cocoa, shortening and vanilla.
- *Check refrigerator* for butter or margarine, mayonnaise, catsup, milk, eggs and garlic cloves.

Recipes

SAUCES

Purchase 2 to 3 different sauces to serve with meat. Choices include chili or salsa sauce, chutney, sweet-sour sauce, mustard sauce, steak sauce, pickle relish (regular or hot) or horseradish sauce. Serve each sauce in a separate bowl.

NEW YEAR'S EVE

Beef Fondue Menu, continued

BEEF FONDUE *(4 servings)*

1 (14 1/2-ounce) can chicken broth *(not condensed)*
2 cups 100% white grape juice
1 medium onion, thinly sliced
3 stalks celery, chopped
2 cloves garlic, chopped
1/2 teaspoon pepper
1 teaspoon salt
1 teaspoon dried tarragon
3 sprigs fresh parsley
1 bay leaf
2 pounds beef sirloin, cut into 1-inch cubes**

Two days before serving, heat chicken broth, white grape juice, onion, celery, garlic, salt, pepper, tarragon, parsley and bay leaf to boiling. Cool, cover and refrigerate until serving time. Arrange meat on platter. Strain broth mixture. Place in saucepan and heat to boiling. Carefully pour into fondue pot* and keep warm. Each guest uses his/her own fondue fork to spear meat and place in fondue pot. Cook meat 30 to 60 seconds. Remove meat from fondue pot and transfer to dinner fork before dipping into sauce.
* *A metal fondue pot and burner and 4 fondue forks are necessary for this meal. Allow one fondue pot for every 4 people.*
** *For ease in cubing beef, freeze slightly.*

SPINACH SALAD *(5 to 6 servings)*

DRESSING

1/4 cup cider vinegar
1/3 cup catsup
1 tablespoon Worcestershire sauce
1/2 cup sugar
1 cup vegetable oil

SALAD

6 cups fresh spinach
3 tomatoes, cut into wedges
1 bunch green onions, sliced
1 (8-ounce) can sliced water chestnuts, drained
4 slices bacon, crisply cooked, broken into 1/2-inch pieces

In a jar with a tight-fitting lid, combine all dressing ingredients; shake well. Refrigerate until ready to serve. Wash spinach in cold water; drain well and dry in paper towels or use a salad spinner. Tear into bite-size pieces. Combine all salad ingredients in large bowl. Just before serving, toss with enough dressing to coat all ingredients well.

(continued, next page)

NEW YEAR'S EVE

Beef Fondue Menu, continued

PARMESAN CHEESE BREAD *(10 to 12 servings)*

1 loaf French bread
1/4 cup butter, softened
3/4 cup mayonnaise
1/2 cup Parmesan cheese
1/3 cup finely chopped onion
1 teaspoon Worcestershire sauce
Paprika

Heat oven to 300 degrees. Cut bread in half lengthwise. Spread butter on cut surfaces of bread. Place on cookie sheet; put in oven to warm. Combine mayonnaise, Parmesan cheese, onion and Worcestershire sauce. Remove bread from oven. Turn oven to 375 degrees. Spread cheese mixture on cut surfaces of bread. Sprinkle with paprika. Bake 10 to 15 minutes or until thoroughly heated. Slice and serve. Bread can be wrapped in foil to keep warm, if necessary.

CHOCOLATE CAKE *(12 servings)*

1 3/4 cups all-purpose flour
2 teaspoons baking powder
1/2 teaspoon baking soda
1/4 teaspoon salt
1/2 cup unsweetened cocoa
1 1/2 cups sugar
1/2 cup plus 2 tablespoons shortening
1/2 cup warm water
2/3 cup milk
2 eggs
1 teaspoon vanilla

Heat oven to 350 degrees. Grease and lightly flour 13x9x2-inch pan. In large bowl, combine flour, baking powder, soda, salt, cocoa and sugar. Add remaining ingredients and beat on low speed with electric mixer until all ingredients are moistened. Increase speed to medium; beat 3 minutes. Use a rubber scraper to scrape sides of bowl. Pour batter into prepared pan. Bake 30 to 35 minutes or until toothpick inserted near center of cake comes out clean. Cool. Frost cooled cake with Cocoa Frosting, below.

COCOA FROSTING

3 1/2 cups powdered sugar
1/2 cup unsweetened cocoa
1/2 cup margarine or butter, melted
1 teaspoon vanilla
5 to 6 tablespoons milk

In large bowl, combine powdered sugar, cocoa, margarine, vanilla and half the milk. Slowly add enough of remaining milk to make a spreading consistency.

NEW YEAR'S EVE

GUEST LIST

Name	Address	Phone Number

EASTER DINNER

Baked Ham

> Glazed Baked Ham
> au Gratin Potatoes
> Rhubarb Gelatin Salad
> Fresh Asparagus
> Cloverleaf Rolls
> Mint Dessert
> Flavored Coffee

MEAL PREPARATION SCHEDULE

The day before, prepare salad and dessert; refrigerate until serving time. About 2 hours before serving, start baking ham. Prepare au Gratin Potatoes and start baking 1 1/4 hours before serving time. Set table. Prepare glaze and glaze ham. Wash and prepare asparagus. Slice ham.

Preparation Time: Ham takes about 10 minutes to prepare and 1 3/4 hours to bake; Au Gratin Potatoes take about 15 minutes to prepare and 60 to 75 minutes to bake; salad takes 20 minutes to prepare; asparagus takes 15 minutes to prepare and 15 minutes to cook; dessert takes 20 to 25 minutes to prepare and must be refrigerated.

SHOPPING LIST

- 3- to 4-pound fully cooked boneless ham
- 1 (32-ounce) package frozen hash-brown potatoes
- 1 (8-ounce) package (2 cups) shredded Cheddar cheese
- 1 (12-ounce) can evaporated skimmed milk(+)

SHOPPING LIST, *continued*

- About 2 pounds fresh rhubarb
- 1 (6-ounce) package strawberry-flavored gelatin
- 1 bunch celery(+)
- 3 to 3 1/2 pounds fresh asparagus
- 1 to 1 1/2 dozen cloverleaf rolls (bakery)
- 1 (12-ounce) package vanilla wafers
- 1 (8-ounce) package Kraft party mints or butter mints
- 1 pint whipping cream
- 1 (10 1/2-ounce) package miniature marshmallows(+)
- Green food color, if desired(+)
- 1/2 pound coffee (*e.g. French Vanilla*)
- *Check cupboard* for brown sugar, dry mustard, vinegar, salt, bread crumbs and granulated sugar.
- *Check refrigerator* for lemon juice, margarine or butter.
- Flower centerpiece (spring flowers, arranged low to the table)

(+) *indicates that this is the smallest size available; there will be leftovers.*

Recipes

GLAZED BAKED HAM *(10 servings)*

3- to 4-pound fully cooked boneless ham
3/4 cup packed brown sugar
1 teaspoon dry mustard
1 tablespoon vinegar

EASTER DINNER

Baked Ham Menu, continued

Place ham fat side up in pan. (Insert meat thermometer if you have one.) Bake at 325 degrees for 1 1/4 hours. In small bowl, combine remaining ingredients to make glaze. Remove ham from oven; score top of ham by making shallow cuts in diamond shapes. Using a spoon, spoon and spread glaze over ham. Return to oven and bake 20 to 30 minutes longer. (Meat thermometer should register 130 degrees.) Let ham stand, covered, for 10 to 15 minutes before carving. Slice and serve.

AU GRATIN POTATOES *(10 to 12 servings)*

1 (32-ounce) package frozen hash-brown potatoes, thawed
1 (8-ounce) package (2 cups) shredded Cheddar cheese
1 teaspoon salt
1 cup evaporated skimmed milk
1/4 cup dry bread crumbs

Grease 2-quart casserole. Alternate layers of potatoes and cheese in casserole. Sprinkle with salt; pour evaporated milk over layers. Sprinkle with bread crumbs. Bake at 325 degrees for 60 to 75 minutes.

RHUBARB GELATIN SALAD *(8 to 10 servings)*

3 cups diced fresh rhubarb
1/2 cup sugar
1 (6-ounce) package strawberry-flavored gelatin
2 cups cold water
1 1/2 cups finely diced celery
1/4 cup lemon juice

Combine rhubarb and sugar in medium saucepan; cook over low heat until rhubarb is tender. Do not stir. Turn up heat and quickly heat mixture to boiling. Remove from heat; gently stir in gelatin until dissolved. Stir in remaining ingredients. Pour into a 9x9-inch pan; refrigerate until serving time.

ASPARAGUS *(8 to 10 servings)*

Break off tough ends as far down as stalks snap easily. Wash asparagus in cold water. Cut spears into 1-inch pieces. Cook lower stalk pieces in 1 inch boiling salted water (1/2 teaspoon salt/cup of water) about 6 minutes. Add tips; cook until crisp tender, about 5 minutes. Drain. Place in serving bowl; dot with butter, if desired.

(continued, next page)

EASTER DINNER

Baked Ham Menu, continued

MINT DESSERT *(12 to 15 servings)*

1 (12-ounce) package vanilla wafers
1/2 cup margarine, melted
1 (8-ounce) package party mints or butter mints
1 pint whipping cream
1/2 (10 1/2-ounce) package miniature marshmallows
Few drops green food color, if desired

Crush vanilla wafers in blender or food processor, or place in plastic bag and roll with rolling pin until crushed. Combine crumbs with margarine. Reserve 1 cup of mixture for topping. Pat remaining crumbs on bottom of 13x9x2-inch pan or rectangular plastic container. Crush mints. Whip cream until stiff peaks form. Gently stir mints, marshmallows and food color into whipped cream until thoroughly blended. Spread over crumb crust in pan. Sprinkle with reserved crumbs. Refrigerate several hours or overnight. Cut and serve on dessert plates.

"They have pierced my hands."
Psalm 22:16

EXTRA MENUS OR RECIPES

Paste a gift-card envelope here
to store extra recipes

FOURTH OF JULY

Hamburgers and Brats

Grilled Hamburgers and Bratwurst
Layered Lettuce Salad
Watermelon Wedges
Dirt Dessert
Iced Tea

MEAL PREPARATION SCHEDULE

The night before, prepare Layered Lettuce Salad; cover and refrigerate. The night before or early on the 4th, prepare Dirt Dessert; cover and refrigerate. Make instant tea or use tea bags; follow directions on jar or package and refrigerate. One hour before serving, start grill. Cook brats in malt beverage. While brats are cooking, cut watermelon into wedges and shape hamburger patties. Begin grilling hamburgers and brats about 10 minutes before serving. Serve iced tea with lemon slices and sugar.

Preparation Time: Layered Salad takes 20 to 25 minutes to prepare. Dirt Dessert takes 20 to 30 minutes to prepare; hamburgers 10 minutes to prepare and 10 minutes to grill; brats take 5 minutes to prepare and 25 minutes to cook; watermelon takes 15 minutes to prepare.

SHOPPING LIST

- 2 pounds lean ground beef
- 1 package of 6 uncooked bratwurst
- 1 (12-ounce) can nonalcoholic malt beverage
- 1 medium head lettuce

SHOPPING LIST, *continued*

- 1 bunch celery(+)
- 1 large green bell pepper
- 1 medium red onion
- 1 (4-ounce) package shredded Cheddar cheese(+)
- 1 (8-ounce) package sliced bacon(+)
- 1 package of 8 hamburger buns
- 1 package of 8 bratwurst buns(+)
- 1/2 watermelon
- 1 (16-ounce) jar mayonnaise
- 1 (8-ounce) package cream cheese
- 2 (3 1/2-ounce) packages vanilla instant pudding mix
- 1 quart milk
- 1 (16-ounce) container frozen whipped topping
- 1 (20-ounce) package chocolate sandwich cookies
- 1 new (clean) 8-inch flower pot
- 15 to 20 gummi worms, if desired
- 1 garden trowel, if desired
- Instant tea or tea bags
- 1 lemon
- *Check cupboard* for salt, pepper, powdered sugar and granulated sugar.
- *Check refrigerator* for butter or margarine.

(+) *indicates that this is the smallest size available; there will be leftovers.*

Recipes

GRILLED HAMBURGERS *(8 servings)*

2 pounds lean ground beef
1 teaspoon salt
1/8 teaspoon pepper
8 hamburger buns

FOURTH OF JULY

Hamburgers and Brats Menu, continued

Gently combine ground beef, salt and pepper. Shape into 8 patties about 3/4-inch thick. Place on grill about 4 inches above coals. Grill for 4 to 6 minutes; turn patties and grill for 4 to 6 minutes longer or until done. Serve on hamburger buns.

BRATWURST *(6 servings)*

1 package of 6 uncooked bratwurst
1 (12-ounce) can nonalcoholic malt beverage
8 bratwurst buns

Pour malt beverage into large skillet. Add brats and heat to boiling over medium-high heat. Reduce heat to low, cover and simmer about 15 minutes. Remove brats from skillet using tongs. Grill for 4 to 5 minutes per side or until brown. Serve on brat buns.

LAYERED LETTUCE SALAD *(10 servings)*

1 head lettuce, torn into bite-size pieces
1 cup chopped celery
1 large green bell pepper, chopped
1 medium red onion, sliced
1 3/4 cups mayonnaise
2 tablespoons sugar
3 ounces (3/4 cup) shredded Cheddar cheese
8 slices bacon, crisply cooked and crumbled*

Place lettuce in large salad bowl or 13x9x2-inch baking dish or pan. Add layers of celery, green pepper and onion, in that order, over lettuce. Combine mayonnaise and sugar; spread over layers in bowl. Sprinkle cheese, then bacon over mayonnaise. Cover with plastic wrap; refrigerate overnight. Just before serving, toss salad.
* To cook bacon in a microwave, place paper towel on microwave-safe bacon rack. Place bacon on paper towel; cover with another paper towel. Microwave on HIGH for 8 to 9 minutes or until bacon is done.

DIRT DESSERT *(8 to 10 servings)*

1 (20-ounce) package chocolate sandwich cookies
1 (8-ounce) package cream cheese
1/2 cup butter, softened
1 cup powdered sugar
2 (3 1/2-ounce) packages vanilla instant pudding mix

3 1/2 cups milk
1 (16-ounce) container frozen whipped topping, thawed
1 new (clean) 8-inch flower pot
15 to 20 gummi worms, if desired
1 garden trowel, if desired

Finely crush cookies between 2 sheets of waxed paper with a rolling pin or in a food processor with a metal blade; set aside. To soften cream cheese in microwave, remove cheese from wrapper; place in microwave-safe dish. Microwave on DEFROST for 30 to 40 seconds or until soft. Place softened cheese in bowl. Add butter and powdered sugar to cream cheese. Blend until smooth. In separate bowl, combine pudding mix and milk. Mix until thick and creamy. Add to cream cheese mixture. Fold in whipped topping. Layer crumbs, pudding mixture and gummi worms in flower pot, starting and ending with crumbs. Refrigerate until serving time. Serve with trowel.

"Man must cease attributing his problems to his environment, and learn again to exercise his will—his personal responsibility."

— Albert Schweitzer

CHAPTER VIII

A NIGHT WITH THE BOYS

This will be short. I did not have many nights with the boys. (And those that I did have, I don't want to talk about!) My life as a single man was cut short by marriage in my early twenties, with fatherhood following a couple of years later. The next thirty years were consumed with fulfilling these responsibilities.

While my marriage came to a premature end, my family and fatherhood responsibilities continued on. There were braces, soccer shoes, college expenses and weddings to provide for and participate in. These family functions never end! Indeed, the "duties" of grandfatherhood have recently been added. Pure delight!

In retrospect, I would not change an inch or an hour. While mistakes were made, good things have resulted for all of us. So, instead of "the boys," my family enjoys the following meals. They've yielded fun times!

HOMEMADE PIZZA

Pizza from Scratch

MEAL PREPARATION SCHEDULE

Start pizza dough about 1 hour before serving. After dough is mixed, prepare topping.

Preparation Time: Dough and toppings take 30 to 35 minutes to prepare; 25 minutes to bake.

(+) indicates that this is the smallest size available; there will be leftovers.

SHOPPING LIST

- 1 strip (3 packages) active dry yeast(+)
- 1 pound bulk pork sausage
- 1 small onion
- 1 (8-ounce) can tomato sauce
- 1 (6-ounce) can tomato paste
- Fresh mushrooms, 1 pint(+) or 3 ounces if available in bulk
- 1 (8-ounce) package (2 cups) shredded mozzarella cheese
- *Check cupboard* for salt, sugar, vegetable oil, flour, dried basil leaves, dried oregano leaves and pepper.
- *Check refrigerator* for garlic.

Recipe

PIZZA FROM SCRATCH *(2 [12-inch] pizzas)*

Dough

1 package active dry yeast
1 teaspoon sugar
3/4 cup warm water (110 to 115 degrees)
1 teaspoon salt
2 tablespoons vegetable oil
2 1/2 cups all-purpose flour

Combine yeast, 1 teaspoon sugar and warm water in medium bowl; stir to mix. Let stand a few minutes until yeast is dissolved and mixture begins to foam. Stir in 1 teaspoon salt, oil and 2 cups of the flour. Place dough on well-floured surface. Knead 5 to 10 minutes until smooth and elastic. Knead in remaining flour if necessary to prevent from sticking. Cover dough with plastic wrap while preparing sauce.

Sauce & Topping

1 pound bulk pork sausage
1 small onion, chopped
1 clove garlic, minced
1 (8-ounce) can tomato sauce
1 (6-ounce) can tomato paste
1/3 cup water
1 teaspoon salt
1 teaspoon sugar
1 teaspoon dried basil leaves
1 teaspoon dried oregano leaves
1/8 teaspoon pepper
1 cup sliced, fresh mushrooms
1 (8-ounce) package (2 cups) shredded mozzarella cheese

In skillet over medium heat, cook sausage, onion and garlic until sausage is brown, stirring to break up lumps. Drain off fat. Combine remaining ingredients, except mushrooms and cheese.

Heat oven to 425 degrees. Divide dough in half. Grease two 12-inch pizza pans or medium size cookie sheets. With floured hands, pat half of dough into each pan. Spread each crust with half of sauce mixture; top with half of browned sausage mixture, half of mushrooms and half of cheese. Bake 20 to 25 minutes or until cheese is light brown.

HOMEMADE PIZZA

Whole Wheat Pizza with Vegetable Topping

MEAL PREPARATION SCHEDULE

Thaw bread dough. (See page 43, Teddy Bear Bread recipe.) Pat dough into pan, prepare vegetables.

Preparation Time: About 35 minutes, after bread dough is thawed.

SHOPPING LIST

- 1 package frozen whole wheat bread dough(+)
- 1 cup broccoli pieces (from salad bar)
- 1 cup cauliflower pieces (from salad bar)
- Fresh mushrooms, 1 pint(+) or 3 ounces if available in bulk.

SHOPPING LIST, *continued*

- 1 pound carrots(+)
- 1 (2 1/4-ounce) can sliced, ripe olives
- 1 small red bell pepper
- 1 small yellow bell pepper
- 1 small red onion
- 1 (15-ounce) can tomato sauce
- 1 (8-ounce) package shredded mozzarella cheese
- *Check cupboard* for vegetable oil, dried basil leaves and dried oregano leaves.
- *Check refrigerator* for garlic.

(+) *indicates that this is the smallest size available; there will be leftovers.*

Recipe

WHOLE WHEAT PIZZA *(2 [12-inch] pizzas)*

1 loaf frozen whole wheat bread dough, thawed
2 cloves garlic, minced
1 tablespoon vegetable oil
1 cup broccoli pieces
1 cup cauliflower pieces
1 cup sliced, fresh mushrooms
1 cup shredded carrots
1 (2 1/4-ounce) can sliced, ripe olives, drained
1/4 cup water
1 teaspoon dried basil leaves
1 teaspoon dried oregano leaves
1 small red bell pepper, sliced into rings
1 small yellow bell pepper, sliced into rings
1 small red onion, sliced
1 (15-ounce) can tomato sauce
1 (8-ounce) package (2 cups) shredded mozzarella cheese

Heat oven to 425 degrees. Generously grease two 12-inch pizza pans or medium size cookie sheets. Divide thawed dough in half. On floured surface, roll half of dough into 12-inch circle. Place on greased pan. Repeat with other half of dough.

In large skillet over medium heat, cook garlic in oil a few minutes to soften garlic. Add remaining ingredients, except tomato sauce and cheese. Cook over low heat about 5 minutes, stirring occasionally.

Spread half of tomato sauce evenly over each crust. Distribute half of cooked vegetables evenly over each crust. Sprinkle each with half of cheese. Bake 20 to 25 minutes or until cheese is light brown. *(Note: Olives don't need to be cooked; may be sprinkled on top of cheese.)*

HOMEMADE PIZZA

Fast and Easy Pizza

MEAL PREPARATION SCHEDULE

Have each person make their own.

Preparation Time: About 15 minutes to prepare and 15 minutes to bake.

SHOPPING LIST

- 1 (13-ounce) package English muffins or 6 onion bagels
- 1 (10 1/2-ounce) can or jar pizza sauce
- 1 (3 1/2-ounce) package sliced pepperoni
- 1 (4-ounce) can sliced mushrooms, drained
- 1 (8-ounce) package (2 cups) shredded mozzarella cheese

Recipe

FAST AND EASY PIZZA *(6 servings)*

6 English muffins or onion bagels
1 (10 1/2-ounce) can or jar pizza sauce
1 (3 1/2-ounce) package sliced pepperoni
1 (4-ounce) can sliced mushrooms, drained
1 (8-ounce) package (2 cups) shredded mozzarella cheese

Heat oven to 400 degrees. Toast English muffins. Spread 1 to 2 tablespoons pizza sauce on each muffin or bagel half. Top with pepperoni and mushrooms. Sprinkle with cheese. Place on cookie sheet. Bake about 15 minutes until cheese is light brown.

"Believe you are defeated, believe it long enough, and it is likely to become a fact."
– Norman Vincent Peale

Extra Menus or Recipes

Paste a gift-card envelope here
to store extra recipes

HEARTY HOT SOUP

Vegetable Beef Soup

> Vegetable Beef Soup
> French Bread or Bread Sticks
> Cherry Dessert

MEAL PREPARATION SCHEDULE

Prepare soup; prepare cherry dessert while beef and spices are cooking. Begin to prepare vegetables about 30 minutes before time to add them. Slice and butter French bread, if desired.

Preparation Time: Soup, 25 minutes to prepare; 3 1/2 to 4 hours to cook. Cherry Dessert, 15 minutes to prepare, 25 minutes to bake.

SHOPPING LIST

- 3 pounds beef stew meat
- 1 (20-ounce) can tomato juice
- 2 large potatoes
- 1 bunch celery(+)
- 1 pound carrots(+)
- 1 medium onion
- 2 (16-ounce) cans tomatoes

SHOPPING LIST, *continued*

- 1 (12-ounce) can whole kernel corn
- 1 (16-ounce) can peas
- 1 (21-ounce) can cherry pie filling
- 1 (16-ounce) can pie cherries
- 1 (2-layer) package yellow cake mix
- 1 (6-ounce) package walnut pieces
- 1/2 pint whipping cream or 1 (4-ounce) container frozen whipped topping, if desired
- 1 loaf French bread or 1 package bread sticks
- *Check cupboard* for beef bouillon cubes, salt, dried thyme leaves, pepper, whole allspice and bay leaf.
- *Check refrigerator* for butter or margarine.

(+) indicates that this is the smallest size available; there will be leftovers.

Recipes

VEGETABLE BEEF SOUP *(14 servings)*

3 pounds beef stew meat
5 cups water
1 (20-ounce) can tomato juice
3 beef bouillon cubes or 1 tablespoon
  instant beef bouillon
1 1/2 teaspoons salt
1/4 teaspoon dried thyme leaves
1/4 teaspoon pepper
2 whole allspice

1 bay leaf
2 cups peeled, cubed potatoes
1 cup sliced celery
1 cup sliced carrots
1/2 cup chopped onion
2 (16-ounce) cans tomatoes, cut up
1 (12-ounce) can whole kernel corn
1 (16-ounce) can peas, undrained

Cut beef into bite-size pieces. In large sauce pan or Dutch oven, combine beef, water and tomato juice. Heat to boiling over high heat. Reduce heat to low; cover and simmer 30 minutes. Add bouillon cubes, salt, thyme, pepper, allspice and bay leaf*; cover. Simmer 2 1/2 to 3 hours or until beef is tender. Remove allspice and bay leaf. Add remaining ingredients. Heat to boiling over high heat. Reduce heat to low; cover and simmer 30 minutes or until vegetables are tender.

* Tip: Place allspice and bay leaf in tea ball or tie in small piece of cheesecloth for easy removal.

HEARTY HOT SOUP

Vegetable Beef Soup Menu, continued

CHERRY DESSERT *(12 servings)*

1 (21-ounce) can cherry pie filling
1 (16-ounce) can pie cherries, drained
1 (2-layer) package yellow cake mix
1 cup coarsely chopped walnuts
2/3 cup margarine or butter, melted
Whipped cream or whipped topping, if desired

Heat oven to 350 degrees. Pour pie filling and cherries into 13x9x2-inch pan; stir to mix. Sprinkle dry cake mix and walnuts evenly over cherry mixture. Pour butter over cake. Bake 20 to 25 minutes or until golden brown. Cool. Serve with whipped cream.

"Set your heart on
things above."
Col.3:1

HEARTY HOT SOUP

Chili Menu

Carol's Chili
Quick and Easy Bread
Carrot and Celery Sticks
Brownies

MEAL PREPARATION SCHEDULE

About 3 hours before serving, prepare chili. Clean and cut up carrots and celery sticks; cover with cold water and refrigerate until serving time. About 1 hour before serving, prepare Quick and Easy Bread. While bread is baking, dish up toppings for Chili; cover with waxed paper or plastic wrap and refrigerate until serving time.

Preparation Time: Chili, about 20 minutes to prepare, 3 hours to cook. Quick and Easy Bread, 10 minutes to prepare, 45 minutes to bake. Carrots and celery, about 15 minutes.

SHOPPING LIST

- 2 pounds ground beef
- 1 small onion
- 1 bunch celery(+)
- 1 pound carrots(+)

SHOPPING LIST, *continued*

- 1 (10 3/4-ounce) can condensed tomato soup
- 1 (28-ounce) can whole tomatoes
- 1 (1 1/4-ounce) envelope chili seasoning mix
- 1 (15 1/2-ounce) can red kidney beans
- 2 (15 1/2-ounce) cans chili beans
- 1 (4-ounce) package shredded Cheddar cheese
- 1 (8-ounce) carton dairy sour cream or plain yogurt
- 1 bunch green onions
- 1 (12-ounce) can nonalcoholic malt beverage
- Bakery brownies
- *Check cupboard* for salt, flour, brown sugar, chili powder, grated Parmesan cheese and baking powder.

(+) *indicates that this is the smallest size available; there will be leftovers.*

Recipes

CAROL'S CHILI *(12 servings)*

2 pounds ground beef
1 small onion, diced
2 cups diced celery
1 (10 3/4-ounce) can condensed tomato soup
1 (28-ounce) can whole tomatoes, undrained and cut up
1 (1 1/4-ounce) envelope chili seasoning mix
3 tablespoons chili powder
1 (15 1/2-ounce) can red kidney beans, undrained
2 (15 1/2-ounce) cans chili beans, undrained
Toppings:
    Shredded Cheddar or Monterey jack cheese
    Grated Parmesan cheese
    Dairy sour cream or plain yogurt
    Chopped green onions

Hearty Hot Soup

Chili Menu, continued

In large saucepan or Dutch oven, brown ground beef, onion and celery; drain off fat. Stir in soup, tomatoes, chili seasoning mix and chili powder. Heat to boiling over high heat. Reduce heat, cover and simmer for 2 hours, stirring occasionally. Stir in kidney beans and chili beans. Simmer 20 to 30 minutes or until beans are thoroughly heated. Serve with assorted toppings.

Quick and Easy Bread *(1 loaf)*

3 cups all-purpose flour*
4 1/2 teaspoons baking powder*
1/2 teaspoon salt*
3 tablespoons brown sugar
1 (12-ounce) can nonalcoholic malt beverage

Heat oven to 350 degrees. Grease 9x5x3-inch pan. In medium bowl, combine flour, baking powder, salt and brown sugar. Add half of malt beverage; mix well. Stir in remaining malt beverage just until mixed. Pour into greased pan. Bake 45 to 50 minutes until golden brown and loaf sounds hollow when tapped. Cool 10 minutes; remove from pan. Serve warm.
* *Tip: 3 cups self-rising flour can be substituted for all-purpose flour, baking powder and salt.*

"Be more concerned with your character than with your reputation. Your character is what you really are while your reputation is merely what others think you are."
– John Wooden

BARBECUE

Grilled Chicken and Cheese

> Grilled Chicken and Cheese Sandwiches
> Corn on the Cob
> Three-Bean Salad
> Pickle Spears
> Saint Croix River Bottom Dessert

MEAL PREPARATION SCHEDULE

The night before or early on the day of the barbecue, prepare Three Bean Salad and Saint Croix River Dessert; cover and refrigerate. About 70 minutes before serving time, start charcoal or grill. While heating, flatten chicken and prepare corn for grill. Add chicken the last 10 minutes. About 30 minutes before serving, place corn on grill. Baste or turn according to recipe. Place pickle spears in serving dish.

Preparation Time: Chicken, about 15 minutes to prepare; 10 minutes to grill. Three-Bean Salad, 15 minutes to prepare; chill 2 to 3 hours. Saint Croix River Bottom Dessert, 30 minutes to prepare; chill at least 2 hours. Corn, about 15 minutes to prepare; 30 minutes to grill.

SHOPPING LIST

- 6 skinless, boneless chicken breast halves
- 1 (18-ounce) jar prepared barbecue sauce
- 1 (6-ounce) package sliced cooked ham

SHOPPING LIST, *continued*

- 6 slices Provolone cheese (from deli)
- 6 large crusty hamburger buns
- 6 ears of corn
- 1 (16-ounce) can green beans
- 1 (16-ounce) can wax beans
- 1 (15 1/2-ounce) can red kidney beans
- 1 bunch celery
- 1 small green bell pepper
- 1 red onion
- 1 (24-ounce) jar dill pickle spears
- 1 (8-ounce) package cream cheese
- 1 (4-ounce) package pecan pieces
- 1 (8-ounce) container frozen whipped topping
- 1 (3 1/2-ounce) package chocolate instant pudding mix
- 1 (3 1/2-ounce) package vanilla instant pudding mix
- 1 quart milk
- 1 (4-ounce) milk chocolate candy bar
- *Check cupboard* for salt, pepper, sugar, vinegar, vegetable oil, flour and powdered sugar.
- *Check refrigerator* for butter or margarine.

Recipes

GRILLED CHICKEN AND CHEESE SANDWICHES *(6 servings)*

> 6 skinless, boneless chicken breast halves
> 1 (18-ounce) jar prepared barbecue sauce
> 6 slices Provolone cheese
> 1 (6-ounce) package sliced cooked ham
> 6 large crusty hamburger buns

Start charcoal in grill about 30 minutes ahead of cooking time. Wash chicken and trim off excess fat. Place chicken breasts, one at a time, between pieces of waxed paper; flatten with a rolling pin until about 1/4 inch thick. Place grill about 8 inches from heat; place chicken on grill. Grill 8 to 10 minutes or until juices run clear, brushing with barbecue sauce frequently and turning once.

BARBECUE

Grilled Chicken and Cheese Menu, continued

Place 1 cheese slice on each piece of chicken. When cheese is melted, place 1 ham slice over cheese. Remove chicken from grill; place in buns.

CORN ON THE COB *(6 servings)*

6 ears of sweet corn
Softened butter
Salt and pepper

Husk corn, removing all silk. Wash corn in cold water. Spread each ear with butter; sprinkle with salt and pepper. Wrap each ear in a piece of aluminum foil. Place on grill. Cook about 30 minutes, turning about 4 times during cooking.

THREE-BEAN SALAD *(10 servings)*

1 (16-ounce) can green beans, drained
1 (16-ounce) can wax beans, drained
1 (15 1/2-ounce) can red kidney beans,
   drained
1 cup sliced celery
1 small green bell pepper, sliced

1 red onion, sliced and separated into rings
1/2 cup sugar
1 teaspoon salt
1/4 teaspoon pepper
1/2 cup vinegar
1/4 cup vegetable oil

The night before or early in the day, place beans, celery, green pepper and onion rings in large bowl. Combine remaining ingredients in small bowl; stir well. Pour sugar mixture over vegetable mixture; toss to coat. Cover and refrigerate until serving time.

SAINT CROIX RIVER BOTTOM DESSERT *(12 to 15 servings)*

Crust

3/4 cup butter or margarine, softened
1 1/2 cups all-purpose flour
1 cup chopped pecans

Filling

1 (8-ounce) package cream cheese,
   softened
1 cup powdered sugar

Filling, *continued*

1 (8-ounce) container frozen whipped
   topping, thawed
1 (3 1/2-ounce) package chocolate instant
   pudding mix
1 1/2 cups milk
1 (3 1/2-ounce) package vanilla instant
   pudding mix
1 1/2 cups milk
1 (4-ounce) milk chocolate candy bar

Heat oven to 350 degrees. Combine butter and flour with fork until mixture resembles coarse crumbs. Stir in chopped pecans. Press flour mixture on bottom of 13x9x2-inch pan. Bake for 20 minutes. Cool completely.

Beat cream cheese and powdered sugar together until fluffy; gently stir into mixture half of whipped topping. Spread over crust. Combine chocolate pudding with 1 1/2 cups milk; spread over cream cheese layer. Refrigerate 5 minutes. Combine vanilla pudding with remaining milk; spread over chocolate pudding layer. Refrigerate 5 more minutes. Spread remaining whipped topping over vanilla pudding layer. Shave candy bar with vegetable peeler and sprinkle over whipped topping. Cover and refrigerate for at least 2 hours.

BARBECUE

Barbecued Beef

Barbecued Beef Brisket
Easy-Do Coleslaw
Potato Chips
Make Your Own Sundaes

MEAL PREPARATION SCHEDULE

Meat preparation must begin the night before. Prepare coleslaw while meat is cooking. The sundaes are a fun-to-make dessert; be sure you have enough bowls. You could have each guest bring one or two toppings, either assigned by you or their favorites. Make sure you have a plastic cloth on the table and let everyone dig in!

Preparation Time: Meat, about 20 minutes to prepare; 6 to 7 hours to bake. Coleslaw, about 10 minutes to prepare.

(+) indicates that this is the smallest size available; there will be leftovers.

SHOPPING LIST

- 1 (16-ounce) package shredded cabbage
- 1 pound carrots(+)
- 1 (8-ounce) favorite prepared coleslaw dressing
- 5- to 6-pound boneless beef brisket
- 1 (3 1/2-ounce) bottle liquid smoke
- 1 (18-ounce) bottle hickory barbecue sauce
- 12 to 14 hoagie buns
- 1 (16-ounce) package potato chips
- 1 (5-quart) pail vanilla or 1/2 gallon vanilla plus 1/2 gallon of your favorite flavor ice cream
- Several of the following toppings: chocolate sauce, caramel sauce, marshmallow creme, frozen strawberries, bananas, peanuts or sunflower seeds, whipped cream or frozen whipped topping
- *Check cupboard* for onion salt, garlic salt, celery salt, Worcestershire sauce and brown sugar.

Recipes

EASY-DO COLESLAW *(10 to 12 servings)*

1 (16-ounce) package shredded cabbage
1 cup shredded carrots
1 (8-ounce) bottle of your favorite coleslaw dressing

Place cabbage and carrots in bowl; add dressing to make salad of desired moistness. Cover and refrigerate until serving time.

BARBECUE

Barbecued Beef Menu, continued

BARBECUED BEEF BRISKET *(12 to 14 servings)*

5- to 6-pound boneless beef brisket
1 teaspoon onion salt
1 teaspoon garlic salt
1 teaspoon celery salt
2 tablespoons Worcestershire sauce
1 (3 1/2-ounce) bottle liquid smoke
1 (18-ounce) bottle hickory barbecue sauce
3/4 cup packed brown sugar
12 to 14 hoagie buns

Sprinkle brisket with 1/2 teaspoon onion salt, 1/2 teaspoon garlic salt, 1/2 teaspoon celery salt; rub into meat with your hand. Add 1 tablespoon Worcestershire sauce; rub in. Place brisket in sealable plastic bag. Add 1/2 bottle of liquid smoke; seal plastic bag. Refrigerate several hours or overnight. About 7 hours before serving, open plastic bag and pour off all liquid. Place brisket on large piece of foil; sprinkle with remaining salts, Worcestershire sauce and liquid smoke. Wrap in foil and seal tightly. Place in baking dish or pan to catch any liquid that may leak out. Bake at 250 degrees for 5 to 6 hours (1 hour per pound). Remove meat from oven, increase oven temperature to 350 degrees. Combine barbecue sauce and brown sugar in small bowl. Open foil; pour sauce mixture over baked meat. Return to oven; bake 1 hour longer. Cut meat into thin slices. Serve in hoagie buns.

MAKE YOUR OWN SUNDAES *(12 to 14 servings)*

1 (5-quart) pail vanilla ice cream or
1/2 gallon vanilla and 1/2 gallon any other flavor ice cream
Some topping choices:
    Chocolate sauce, caramel sauce, marshmallow creme, frozen
    strawberries, thawed; sliced bananas, peanuts or sunflower seeds;
    whipped cream or frozen whipped topping

Serve scoops of ice cream in dishes. Let guests top as desired.

"In great attempts it is glorious even to fail."
– Vince Lombardi

"Aggressive fighting for the right is the greatest sport in the world."
— Theodore Roosevelt

CHAPTER IX

WILD GAME DINNERS

Writing this introduction is difficult for me. I'm more of a couch potato than a professional sportsman. Just ask my son and sons-in-law. They love me, but will say, "He's right!" My real interest is wilderness and white-water canoeing. I like the natural quietness and scenery, mixed with the thrill of running the rapids.

However, there have been a few minor hunting episodes in my life. I shot at a deer once, and hit it! But it didn't drop and we never did find it. Squirrel hunting was fun, but no one cared for squirrel meat. Dove hunting was a challenge, but my shotgun accidently discharged one day, nearly killing my best friend. I'm still a bit paranoid.

A quail "hunt" with pen-raised birds was interesting. They didn't know how to fly. The dog and I stumbled upon one standing on the edge of a corn field. It just stood there, shivering, looking up at us with its dark, forlorn eyes like "poor little Tweety Bird" in the cartoons. I didn't have the heart to blow it away.

Forty years ago I went pheasant hunting with my dad and his friend. They used me as the dog! I can still remember standing face-to-face with this bird hiding along the bank of a dry stream bed. I barked! It flew! "Bangity, Bang-Bang, Bang!" They both missed it!

Fishing has always been a time for quiet meditation or fellowship with family and friends, which, to me, is the essence of it all, anyway.

How many men (and women) 20, 40, 60 years old are still waiting for their dad to take them fishing? How many youngsters have been promised a hunting or camping trip only to have their dreams crushed by Dad's "unexpected" business meeting? I shudder to think of the answer. An adventurous time with Dad is precious beyond measure. The memories last a lifetime.

In the event that "something" is brought home, the following menus are provided to celebrate. They are excellent!

Wild Duck Dinner

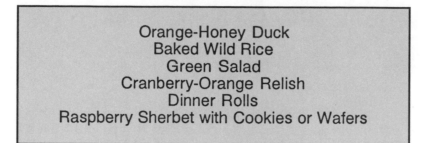

Orange-Honey Duck
Baked Wild Rice
Green Salad
Cranberry-Orange Relish
Dinner Rolls
Raspberry Sherbet with Cookies or Wafers

Meal Preparation Schedule

Start preparing duck about 3 hours before serving. Thaw Cranberry-Orange Relish; place in small dish just before serving. Start preparing Wild Rice about 1 3/4 hours before serving. Prepare salad. Warm rolls if desired. Dish up sherbet at serving time.

Preparation Time: Duck takes about 30 minutes to prepare and 2 1/2 hours to bake. Wild rice takes about 5 minutes to prepare and 1 3/4 hours to bake. Salad takes about 15 minutes to prepare.

Shopping List

- 2 ducks
- 1 orange
- 1 (12-ounce) jar honey(+)
- 1 (6-ounce) can frozen orange juice concentrate(+)
- 1 (16-ounce) package wild rice(+)

Shopping List, *continued*

- 1 (14 1/2-ounce) can chicken broth *(not condensed)*
- Salad greens of your choice (see recipe)
- 1 small cucumber(+)
- 1 bunch green onions(+)
- 1 (8-ounce) bottled salad dressing of your choice(+)
- 1 small package seasoned salad croutons(+)
- 1 (10-ounce) package frozen cranberry-orange relish or 1 (12-ounce) container cranberry orange sauce
- Dinner rolls (from bakery)
- 1 pint raspberry sherbet
- Bakery or homemade cookies or wafers
- *Check cupboard* for dried basil leaves, ground ginger and salt.
- *Check refrigerator* for butter or margarine and lemon juice.

(+) *indicates that this is the smallest size available; there will be leftovers.*

Recipes

Orange-Honey Duck *(2 to 4 servings)*

1 1/2 teaspoons dried basil leaves
1/2 teaspoon ground ginger
1 teaspoon salt
2 ducks (one duck will serve 1 to 2 persons)
1 orange, quartered
1 3/4 cups water
1 cup honey
1/2 cup butter or margarine
2 teaspoons lemon juice
1/2 cup frozen orange juice concentrate, thawed (undiluted)

WILD DUCK DINNER, *continued*

In small bowl, combine basil, ginger and salt; sprinkle over inside and outside of ducks. Place 2 orange quarters in each duck; place ducks, breast side up, in shallow baking or roasting pan.

In saucepan, combine remaining ingredients; heat over low heat until mixture thickens into a syrup. Pour about 1/4 cup of mixture over each duck. Reserve remainder of syrup. Cover. Bake at 350 degrees for 30 minutes.

Turn ducks breast side down. Add more syrup. Cover; reduce oven temperature to 300 degrees. Roast ducks 2 to 2 1/2 hours or until tender. During the last 10 minutes of roasting, turn duck breast side up and spoon reserved syrup over ducks. Remove orange sections before serving.

BAKED WILD RICE *(2 to 3 servings)*

1/2 cup uncooked wild rice, rinsed and drained
1 (14 1/2-ounce) can chicken broth

Combine wild rice and chicken broth in 1-quart casserole. Cover and bake at 300 degrees for 1 hour. Fluff with fork; add small amount of water if necessary. Bake until wild rice is tender, about 40 minutes longer.

GREEN SALAD *(2 servings)*

2 cups salad greens, torn into bite-size pieces
  (iceberg lettuce, spinach, romaine or bibb lettuce)
1/2 small cucumber, sliced
3 to 4 green onions, including tops, sliced
Bottled salad dressing of your choice
Seasoned croutons, if desired

In salad bowl, toss greens, cucumber and onions together. Add dressing; toss again. Sprinkle with croutons.

"No man is good enough to be another man's master."
– George Bernard Shaw

PHEASANT DINNER

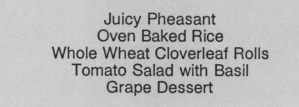

Juicy Pheasant
Oven Baked Rice
Whole Wheat Cloverleaf Rolls
Tomato Salad with Basil
Grape Dessert

MEAL PREPARATION SCHEDULE

Two-and-a-half hours before serving prepare Grape Dessert. Immediately start preparing Pheasant. Prepare Tomato Salad and refrigerate. Forty-five minutes before serving, prepare Rice. Just before serving, add lemon juice to salad.

Preparation Time: Pheasant takes about 20 to 25 minutes to prepare and 1 1/2 hours to simmer. Rice takes about 5 minutes to prepare and 35 minutes to bake. Salad takes about 10 minutes to prepare and 1 hour to chill. Grapes take 10 minutes to prepare and need to stand 2 hours.

(+) indicates that this is the smallest size available; there will be leftovers.

SHOPPING LIST

- 1 pheasant
- 1 (8-ounce) carton whipping cream, if desired
- 4 cloverleaf rolls (from bakery)
- 2 tomatoes
- Fresh basil
- 1 pound seedless red grapes
- 1 quart orange juice or 6-ounce can frozen orange juice concentrate(+)
- 1 (8-ounce) carton dairy sour cream(+)
- *Check cupboard* for salt, baking mix, chicken bouillon cube, rice, vegetable oil and brown sugar.
- *Check refrigerator* for butter or margarine and lemon juice.

Recipes

JUICY PHEASANT *(2 servings)*

1 pheasant
1/2 cup baking mix (Bisquick)
1 1/2 tablespoons butter
1 1/2 tablespoons margarine
1 chicken bouillon cube
1 cup water
Whipping cream, if desired

With a sharp knife, cut pheasant into pieces. Coat each piece with baking mix. In skillet or electric fry pan over medium-high heat, melt butter and margarine. Add pheasant and cook until brown, turning to brown all sides. Let steam 1 to 2 minutes. Dissolve bouillon in water; pour over pheasant. Cover; reduce heat and simmer 1 1/2 hours. (Make gravy by stirring whipping cream into pan juices to desired consistency, if desired.)

PHEASANT DINNER, *continued*

BAKED RICE *(4 servings)*

1 cup uncooked regular rice
1 tablespoon butter
1 teaspoon salt
2 cups boiling water

Heat oven to 350 degrees. In greased 2-quart casserole, combine rice, butter and salt. Stir in water; cover. Bake 35 to 40 minutes.

TOMATO SALAD WITH BASIL *(2 to 3 servings)*

2 tomatoes
1/2 teaspoon salt
1 tablespoon finely chopped fresh basil
1 tablespoon vegetable oil
1 1/2 tablespoons lemon juice

Cut core out of tomatoes; cut tomatoes into wedges. Place tomatoes in bowl; sprinkle lightly with salt. Combine basil and oil; pour over tomatoes. Refrigerate for at least 1 hour to blend flavors. Just before serving, toss with lemon juice.

GRAPE DESSERT *(3 to 4 servings)*

2 cups seedless red grapes
1 teaspoon brown sugar
3/4 cup orange juice
1/2 cup dairy sour cream
1 tablespoon brown sugar

At least 2 hours before serving, wash grapes and place in bowl. Sprinkle with 1 teaspoon brown sugar. Pour orange juice over grapes; let stand at room temperature. In small bowl, combine sour cream and 1 tablespoon brown sugar; refrigerate until serving time. At serving time, spoon grape mixture into stemmed glasses or dishes and top each with a spoonful of sour cream mixture.

QUAIL DINNER

Quail with Glaze
Parsley Buttered Noodles
California Blend Vegetables
Corn Muffins
Creamy Lemon Pie

MEAL PREPARATION SCHEDULE

The night before or early on serving day, prepare Creamy Lemon Pie. About 1 1/2 hours before serving, prepare corn muffins and bake according to package directions. About 1 hour before serving, start preparing quail. About 20 minutes before serving, cook noodles. About 15 minutes before serving, cook vegetables as directed on package. Finish noodle preparation.

Preparation Time: Quail takes about 15 minutes to prepare and 50 minutes to cook and bake. Noodles take about 10 minutes to prepare and 10 minutes to cook. Vegetables take about 10 minutes to cook. Corn Muffins take about 10 minutes to prepare and about 15 minutes to bake. Pie takes about 15 minutes to prepare and 3 to 4 hours to chill.

SHOPPING LIST

- 4 quail
- 1 (10-ounce) jar currant jelly(+)
- 1 (6-ounce) can apple juice
- 1 (10-ounce) package egg noodles(+)
- 1 bunch fresh parsley(+)
- 1 (10-ounce) package frozen California vegetables (broccoli, cauliflower, carrots)
- 1 (8-ounce) package corn muffin mix
- 1 (12-ounce) can frozen pink lemonade concentrate
- 1 (14-ounce) can sweetened condensed milk *(not evaporated)*
- 1 (8-ounce) container frozen whipped topping
- 1 (9-ounce) graham cracker pie shell
- *Check refrigerator* for butter or margarine, lemon juice, milk and eggs.

(+) indicates that this is the smallest size available; there will be leftovers.

Recipes

QUAIL WITH GLAZE *(2 servings)*

1/2 cup butter
4 quail (2 per person)
1/2 cup currant jelly
1/3 cup apple juice
1 tablespoon lemon juice

Heat oven to 325 degrees. In skillet over medium-high heat, melt butter. Continue cooking and stirring until butter is light brown. Place quail in roasting pan; pour browned butter over quail; cover pan (with foil if necessary). Bake 20 minutes.

In small bowl, combine jelly, apple juice and lemon juice. Uncover quail and spoon jelly mixture over quail. Bake uncovered for 20 minutes longer. Spoon juices from pan over quail.

QUAIL DINNER *continued*

PARSLEY BUTTERED NOODLES *(2 servings)*

3 cups uncooked egg noodles
3 sprigs fresh parsley, chopped
2 tablespoons butter

Cook noodles according to package directions. Drain. Combine with parsley and butter. Serve hot.

CREAMY LEMON PIE *(6 servings)*

1 (12-ounce) can frozen pink lemonade concentrate, thawed
1 (14-ounce) can sweetened condensed milk *(not evaporated)*
1 (8-ounce) container frozen whipped topping, thawed
1 (9-ounce) graham cracker pie shell

Combine lemonade concentrate, condensed milk and whipped topping in large mixer bowl with electric mixer, until thoroughly mixed. Spoon filling in pie shell. Refrigerate 3 to 4 hours. Refrigerate any leftovers *(Tip: Leftovers can be frozen.)*

"Lift up your hearts and hands to God."
Lam. 3:41

VENISON DINNER

Venison Roast
Herb Potatoes
Broccoli-Corn Bake
Crescent Rolls
Fruit Cocktail Cake

MEAL PREPARATION SCHEDULE

The night before or early in the day, prepare Fruit Cocktail Cake. Four hours before serving, prepare roast and put in oven. One and one-half hours before serving, prepare and bake Herb Potatoes. Fifty minutes before serving, prepare Broccoli-Corn Bake. About 15 minutes before serving, open crescent rolls, shape dough as directed on package. As soon as roast is done, increase oven temperature to 375 degrees. Bake rolls as directed on package.

Preparation Time: Venison Roast takes about 15 minutes to prepare and 3 1/2 hours to roast. Herb Potatoes take about 15 minutes to prepare and 1 hour to bake. Broccoli-Corn Bake takes about 10 minutes to prepare and 40 minutes to bake. Fruit Cocktail Dessert takes about 15 minutes to prepare and 45 minutes to bake.

(+) *indicates that this is the smallest size available; there will be leftovers.*

SHOPPING LIST

- 3 1/2- to 4-pound venison roast
- 3 medium onions, sliced
- 4 to 5 potatoes
- Fresh chives (available in packages or pots)
- 1 (10-ounce) package frozen chopped broccoli
- 1 (16-ounce) can cream-style corn
- 1 (8-ounce) package saltine crackers *(for crumbs)* or cracker crumbs
- 1 (8-ounce) package refrigerated crescent dinner rolls
- 1 (3-ounce) package nuts
- 1 (15-ounce) can fruit cocktail
- 1 (4-ounce) container frozen whipped topping, if desired
- *Check cupboard* for dried dillweed, flour, granulated sugar, baking soda, salt, and brown sugar.
- *Check refrigerator* for butter or margarine and eggs.

Recipes

VENISON ROAST *(4 to 6 servings)*

3 1/2- to 4-pound venison roast
2 medium onions, sliced

Trim excess fat from venison. Arrange onion slices over and around roast. Place venison in center of large piece of heavy-duty aluminum foil. Close foil and seal by making a double fold at the edge. Place in baking dish or pan to catch any liquid that may leak out. Bake at 325 degrees for 3 1/2 to 4 hours, or until tender. Open foil and remove venison. Slice venison and arrange on platter.

VENISON DINNER, *continued*

HERB POTATOES *(4 to 5 servings)*

4 to 5 potatoes
1/3 cup butter or margarine, melted
1 tablespoon chopped fresh chives
1/2 teaspoon dried dillweed

Peel and slice potatoes. Place in ungreased 2-quart casserole. Pour butter over potatoes. Sprinkle with herbs. Bake at 325 degrees for 60 to 70 minutes or until tender. Baste 2 or 3 times with margarine from casserole dish.

BROCCOLI-CORN BAKE *(6 servings)*

1 (10-ounce) package frozen chopped broccoli
1/4 cup finely chopped onion
2 tablespoons butter or margarine
1 (16-ounce) can cream-style corn
1 egg
1/2 cup coarse cracker crumbs

Place frozen broccoli and chopped onion in 1 1/2-quart casserole. Cover and microwave on HIGH for 6 to 7 minutes. Drain. Stir in remaining ingredients. Mix well. Bake at 325 degrees for 40 minutes.

FRUIT COCKTAIL CAKE *(9 servings)*

Topping

1/2 cup packed brown sugar
1/3 cup flour
1/2 cup chopped nuts
Whipped topping, if desired

Cake

1 cup all-purpose flour
1 cup sugar
1 teaspoon baking soda
1/4 teaspoon salt
1 (15-ounce) can fruit cocktail *(do not drain)*
1 egg

Heat oven to 350 degrees. Grease 9x9x2-inch pan. In small bowl, combine topping ingredients (except whipped topping); set aside. In large bowl, combine 1 cup flour, sugar, baking soda and salt. Stir in fruit cocktail and liquid. Stir in egg until well mixed. Pour into pan. Sprinkle brown sugar mixture over cake. Bake 40 to 45 minutes or until toothpick inserted in center comes out clean. Remove from oven; cool on rack. Cut into squares and serve with whipped topping.

WALLEYE PIKE DINNER

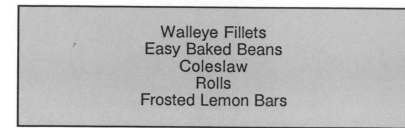

Walleye Fillets
Easy Baked Beans
Coleslaw
Rolls
Frosted Lemon Bars

MEAL PREPARATION SCHEDULE

The night before or early in the day prepare Lemon Bars and Coleslaw. Place fish in refrigerator the night before to start thawing. About 1 hour before serving, prepare and cook Baked Beans. Cut lemon. About 1/2 hour before serving, start fish preparation.

Preparation Time: Walleye Fillets take about 20 minutes to prepare and 10 to 15 minutes to cook. Baked Beans take 10 minutes to prepare and about 40 minutes to bake. Cole Slaw takes about 15 minutes to prepare and 2 to 3 hours to chill. Lemon Bars take about 5 minutes to prepare, 20 minutes to bake and 30 minutes to cool before frosting.

(+) indicates that this is the smallest size available; there will be leftovers.

SHOPPING LIST

- 4 to 5 small or 2 to 3 large walleye fillets, per person
- 1 (8-ounce) box saltine crackers(+)
- 1 (32 to 64-ounce) bottle vegetable oil
- 2 lemons
- 1 (8-ounce) jar tartar sauce, if desired
- 2 (16-ounce) cans pork and beans
- 1 small onion
- 1 (14-ounce) bottle barbecue sauce(+)
- 1 (16-ounce) package shredded cabbage
- 1 large green bell pepper
- Bakery rolls
- 1 (16-ounce) package "one-step" angel food cake mix
- 1 (22-ounce) can lemon pie filling
- 1 (3-ounce) cream cheese, softened
- *Check cupboard* for flour, pepper, white vinegar, sugar, celery seed, dry mustard and powdered sugar.
- *Check refrigerator* for eggs, milk, butter or margarine and lemon juice.

Recipes

WALLEYE FILLETS *(5 to 6 servings)*

Walleye fillets, thawed (4 to 5 small fillets or 2 to 3 large fillets per person)

Vegetable oil for frying *(amount depends on pan size)*

JIM'S FISH BATTER

1/2 cup all-purpose flour
1/4 teaspoon pepper
3 eggs
1/3 cup milk
1 1/2 cups saltine cracker crumbs

Combine flour and pepper in pie plate or other shallow dish. In bowl, combine eggs and milk with wire whisk. Place cracker crumbs in another dish. Dip fillets into flour mixture, turning to cover both sides. Shake off any excess flour. Dip fillets into egg mixture, then into crumbs, covering completely. In large heavy skillet or deep-fat fryer, heat oil to 350 degrees. Place fillet into hot oil; cook 2 to 3 minutes or until golden brown. Place fillet on paper towel to drain. Repeat with remaining fillets. Serve hot with lemon slices and tartar sauce, if desired.

WALLEYE PIKE DINNER, *continued*

EASY BAKED BEANS *(6 to 8 servings)*

2 (16-ounce) cans pork and beans
1 small onion, chopped
1 teaspoon dry mustard
1/3 cup bottled barbecue sauce

Grease 1 1/2- or 2-quart casserole. Combine all ingredients. Bake at 350 degrees for 40 to 45 minutes or until thoroughly heated.

COLESLAW *(8 servings)*

1 (16-ounce) package shredded cabbage
1 large green bell pepper, chopped
1 cup white vinegar
1/2 cup water
1 1/4 cups sugar
1 teaspoon celery seed
1/2 teaspoon dry mustard

In large bowl, combine cabbage and green pepper; set aside. In large saucepan, combine remaining ingredients; heat to boiling. Boil 1 minute; cool. Pour dressing over cabbage mixture. Stir well. Refrigerate at least 2 to 3 hours or until serving time.

FROSTED LEMON BARS *(50 [2x1 1/2-inch] bars)*

1 (16-ounce) package "one-step" angel food cake mix
1 (22-ounce) can lemon pie filling
Frosting:
   2 cups powdered sugar
   1/4 cup butter or margarine, softened
   1 (3-ounce) package cream cheese, softened
   2 tablespoons lemon juice

Heat oven to 350 degrees. Grease 15x10x1-inch jelly roll pan. Combine dry angel food mix with lemon pie filling; spread in greased pan. Bake about 20 minutes or until light brown. Cool.

Combine all frosting ingredients; beat at medium speed until smooth and spreading consistency. Spread over bars. Cut into bars. Store in refrigerator.

Success

"To laugh often and much; to win the respect of intelligent people and affection of children; to earn the appreciation of honest critics and endure the betrayal of false friends; to appreciate beauty, to find the best in others; to leave the world a bit better, whether by a healthy child, a garden patch or a redeemed social condition; to know even one life has breathed easier because you have lived. This is to have succeeded."

— Ralph Waldo Emerson

Menu Index

RECIPE INDEX

RECIPE INDEX, *continued*

RECIPE INDEX, *continued*

RECIPE INDEX, *continued*

ADDITIONAL RECIPES

ADDITIONAL RECIPES

ADDITIONAL RECIPES

ADDITIONAL RECIPES

ADDITIONAL RECIPES

ADDITIONAL RECIPES

ADDITIONAL RECIPES

ADDITIONAL RECIPES

ADDITIONAL RECIPES

ADDITIONAL RECIPES

ADDITIONAL RECIPES

ADDITIONAL RECIPES

ADDITIONAL RECIPES

ADDITIONAL RECIPES

ADDITIONAL RECIPES